GARDEN DESIGN

Kenneth Midgley
GARDEN DESIGN

Prepared in conjunction and collaboration with
the Royal Horticultural Society
Revised and expanded edition

PELHAM BOOKS

ACKNOWLEDGEMENTS

I wish to thank the Royal Horticultural Society for inviting me to write this book. I am conscious of the honour, and I am particularly grateful to Elspeth Napier for her help in checking the nomenclature of plants for this new edition.

I am grateful to my clients and the other generous owners who have made it possible for all of us to see their gardens; and I would also like to thank Muriel Gascoin and the staff of Pelham Books for their help in preparing this revised and expanded edition.

I owe thanks to my wife, Gwen, who is also my assistant, for her help in discussion, criticism and reading the book for the press.

PELHAM BOOKS

Published by the Penguin Group
27 Wrights Lane, London W8 5TZ, England
Viking Penguin, a division of Penguin Books USA Inc.
375 Hudson Street, New York, NY 10014, USA
Penguin Books Australia Ltd, Ringwood, Victoria, Australia
Penguin Books Canada Ltd, 10 Alcorn Avenue, Suite 300, Toronto, Ontario, Canada M4V 3B2
Penguin Books (NZ) Ltd, 182-190 Wairau Road, Auckland 10, New Zealand

Penguin Books Ltd, Registered Offices: Harmondsworth, Middlesex, England

First published in paperback by Penguin Books Ltd 1966
Reissued as a hardback edition by Pelham Books Ltd 1977
Revised, enlarged and expanded edition published by Pelham Books Ltd 1984
Reprinted in paperback 1986, 1987, 1991

1 2 3 4 5 6 7 8 9 10

Copyright © Kenneth Midgley 1966, 1977, 1984

Cataloguing in Publication Data
Midgley, Kenneth 19--
  Garden design
  1. Garden design 2. Gardening
  1. Title
  712'.6 SB473
ISBN 0 7207 1685 3

Typeset by MS Filmsetting Ltd, Frome.
Printed and bound in Singapore by Kyodo Printing Co Pte Ltd

Frontispiece: The white background of the house is a perfect foil for the climbing roses and herbaceous plants at the base of the wall.

CONTENTS

INTRODUCTION

Good design applied to present-day living makes an invaluable contribution to our well-being and to our enjoyment of the things around us. It is a condition we are inclined to take for granted. We tend to overlook the inspiration and effort which go into the making of even the simplest of articles in everyday use. To appreciate this one has only to imagine an unhappy world devoid of all aesthetic design. That elegant kettle, so gracefully styled that one almost forgets that it is also useful, would be a mere container for the efficient heating of water. The imagination if allowed full rein can produce a gruesome picture of functional efficiency and man-made ugliness.

Fortunately, however, the average young couple setting up home today can draw on the work of an unseen army of industrial designers. They may make no claim to any particular degree of artistic appreciation, but will take the greatest care in the selection of their furnishings, rejecting something by one manufacturer in favour of that by another, because the shape and styling pleases them more. If fortunate enough to have a choice of houses available to them, they will show a keen interest in the architecture of the building itself. Results between one pair of home-makers and another will differ, but the process of arriving at the results is the same – the exciting and satisfying process of thoughtful planning.

It is when they come to deal with that part of the home outside the four walls of the house – the plot of land – that reactions seem to vary. The mental approach to garden-making will be affected by a number of factors, but chiefly I suggest by the following.

Most seriously by their interest in gardening; while a complete lack of interest will result in no garden at all, enthusiasm will produce one under the most adverse conditions.

Secondly, there is the matter of funds available. Too often the provision of plants and material is overlooked in the overall budget, or the sum allotted is so disproportionately small that it is impossible, for instance, to enlist outside labour. Nevertheless, provided they are willing to work themselves and to have patience, lack of funds should not be a deterrent. The work will simply take longer, and many of their plants may be given by friends, or grown from seed or cuttings.

The third, and most important factor, and one which has a direct bearing on their confidence, is difficult to put into a few words. It might be described as the ability to appreciate the true nature and purpose of a garden, to see their objective, and to know what it is that they are making.

From my own observation I suggest that a great many would-be garden-

Opposite: Garden archway with ivy, Cotinus, silver foliage, etc.

makers, lacking guidance, take one or both of two courses. They drift from one good idea to another, doing work as the need arises, a path, a bed, a greenhouse and so on, wasting energy and money because there is no coordination of ideas towards a final goal. Alternatively, they will take a photograph which they like from some magazine and try to tear it from its context – often a wider setting – and force it into their own small plot.

The study of photographs – or, better still, actual gardens – is excellent, but it should be done with some understanding of the underlying fundamentals which make them appealing. Knowing how carefully furniture for the house was chosen and the thought which went into the production of a balanced and satisfying arrangement, it must follow that a specially admired garden cannot arise by accident.

It must surely be due to the application, consciously or otherwise, of certain principles which can be sought out and used again. Then an idea can be adapted, the stumbling block of size overcome and a feature from a larger garden modified and reborn successfully in the smaller one. The wealthy land-owner of the past made beautiful gardens and created his own landscape according to a carefully prepared scheme. This, incidentally, is something which we today should be glad of, since much of the countryside we enjoy was made by the landscape architects of the eighteenth century.

What is often overlooked, however, is the simple fact that garden-making, like many other human activities, has had to adapt itself to our changing social structure. As the stately homes and broadacres unhappily grow fewer, a new race of land-owners appears with members holding not 100 hectares, or even 10, but a tenth ($\frac{1}{4}$ acre) and less. These small sites are vitally important. It is in them that we must create *our* havens, though without attempting to emulate the grandeur of a bygone age. We can, however, look and learn, and by assimilating, find the inspiration to organize our own limited outdoor space for use and beauty in a manner consistent with the size of our property and the depth of our pocket. Just as many of the fine gardens of the past remain to be admired, and become monuments to the elegance and taste of their respective periods, so the modern scaled-down counterpart, each a potential gem, will be our contribution to the story of gardening.

There are two questions home-makers must ask themselves. Is the arrangement of their garden as important to them as the house and its contents? Is it reasonable and necessary to give it the same thought and care to achieve the same satisfying results? An affirmative to each will establish a good case for garden design.

Note: In this edition, both imperial and metric units are given, but the conversions are in most cases approximate, since I have tried to give the most natural figure depending upon the unit of measurement the reader wishes to use.

1 FUNDAMENTALS: THE DESIGNER'S TASK

Since this book has been written to help the real beginner with a little plot, as well as the more experienced gardener, I hope the latter will bear with me if some space is devoted to fundamentals, the appreciation of which can not always be taken for granted.

THE SITE

A garden must be individual to the property to which it belongs and to the people who live in it.

Building plots on a plan may look alike, but there is always a subtle difference, either in surroundings, aspect, slope, direction of view, or the need for screening, and there is certainly a difference in people. The garden will develop according to the dictates of the former and the wishes of the latter, and it is not always easy to reconcile the two.

The designer's first duty therefore is to consider carefully his own aims and weigh them against the characteristics of the plot, some of which will help him, while others may hinder or even prevent the execution of his ideas.

Such simple factors as the relationship of the house to neighbouring buildings, and the aspect of the site will together create problems of permanent shadow, and will affect the placing of beds and borders. The quality and type of soil – sandy, gravelly, clay, acid or alkaline – the local climatic conditions, and the presence of industrial air pollution, will affect the choice of plants to be grown. Slope or undulation of the ground will add interest and opportunities of originality, and a natural feature such as the odd tree can give focus to a garden scheme.

Quiet consideration on the site will lead to a thorough knowledge of its potential and its limitations and it is then essential to consider one's aims.

THE PURPOSE OF THE GARDEN

A designer, whatever he may be called upon to produce, will want to know the function, the material to be used, and the probable cost. In our case, for realistic reasons, cost and materials are important, but will be best considered as we go along. Let us first look for an answer to the question on function – 'What is a garden?' 'What is it for?' Posed to a group of people, this question would produce a variety of replies.

The Garden in Relation to the House

One would be that the object is to make a setting for the house; indeed, there are some who would go so far as to say that, if the layout is architecturally in harmony with the building, the

Pool and garden
complementing architecture
of house.

Right: A brick wall provides a
foil for roses in this small
town garden.

Opposite, above: In this
Cotswold garden, the turf
provides a green carpet in
front of the house.

Opposite, below: In this
garden the strong shapes of
the group of conifers repeat
the vertical accents of the
architecture.

planting is of minor importance. The design must, of course, integrate the house with its surroundings, the former being the dominant feature, its salient points being picked up in the shaping of the garden, so that the two become one harmonious unit. But I would never subscribe to the idea that the planting be regarded as a frill or the icing on a cake. Bricks and masonry have a part to play, especially near the building, but they should be used less for their own sake than in conjunction with planting, so that each medium complements the other. How often, for instance, have you see an intrinsically beautiful wall come to life when hung with a filigree of clematis foliage or fronted with a mass of delphiniums?

Plants are the essential components from which gardens are made. Think of the inestimable value of turf (which is a mat of closely grown grass plants), forming a green carpet on which the house stands. Think of low, billowing shrubs nursing the base of the building; the soft outline of hardwood trees contrasting with the harder lines of the roof, the smaller trees visually supporting the walls; the strong shapes of formal cypresses repeating the vertical accents of the architecture, and groups or drifts of plants, from the smallest prostrate shrub to the loftiest tree, to guide where you walk. That is how plants, intelligently used, can serve us in making a setting for the house.

The Vegetable Grower's Garden

One other, obvious answer to our question, and one diametrically opposed to the previous idea, is that a garden is 'A place where we grow things'.

This would be the view of the man whose main interest is the production

of vegetables. He will, in his planning, be guided not so much by aesthetic aims as by the practical considerations of siting and easy working. He is likely therefore to keep his vegetable plot separate from the rest of the garden, except in a very restricted space when he must contrive a siting that is both practical and artistic.

The Collector's Garden

The plant collector would be another thinking in terms of ideal growing conditions, at the expense (if necessary) of aesthetic design. Many an Alpine-plant enthusiast, for example, will appreciate the way in which natural rockwork can form part of the general garden picture, but he will not be unduly concerned as long as *his* stone is arranged to provide a physically suitable home for his plants.

The Family Man's Garden

To many people the garden is a private enclosure designed to cope with the recreational needs of a growing family and their pets; the essentials will be security, privacy, clean firm paths for tricycles, and plenty of open space devoid of 'precious' beds and borders.

Indeed, can one have a garden and dogs? A great many people would say 'No' and resign themselves to scorched grass, burnt conifers and plants which have been flattened by boisterous animals. However, one has only to see a country garden where the owner has a pair of gundogs that know exactly what they may and may not do, for the infinite patience required in training to seem worthwhile.

Young children can also present the keen gardener with problems. One solution is to give toddlers an enclosure in view of the house windows, fenced in with nylon netting supported on canes. The enclosure should be quite plain and uncluttered and at some focal point, relative to the house, a sandpit might be dug.

To avoid the children digging up worms, the pit should be lined with strong polythene, punctured to allow

Below, left: Design for children's play-area near the house.

Below, right: When no longer needed, the play-area can be developed as a garden within the garden.

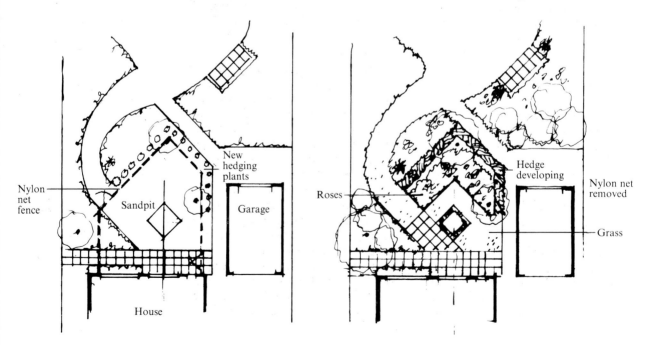

Nylon net fence · Sandpit · New hedging plants · Garage · House

Roses · Hedge developing · Nylon net removed · Grass

drainage. Bearing in mind that a sand-pit is a temporary structure, the most satisfactory method is to draw the polythene over a cut edge of turf and then bury the spare material in a trench alongside the shape of the pit. The use of bricks or stone should be avoided: the safety of the children is more important than neat copings and sharp edges. Anyone able to find in a scrapyard an old tractor or scraper tyre might consider placing it on a sheet of polythene on turf or paving and filling it with sand. Apart from being a sympathetic material, it forms a good seat and for those who like wielding a paintbrush it could be painted white.

The enclosure should be of a size that will allow small children to run about and, if circumstances demand, carpeted with artificial turf. A swing and seesaw could also be included.

The play area should be designed with future development in mind so that when the children have outgrown their special enclosure it can be turned into a little separate garden. Outside the nylon netting could be planted a hedge that would be growing while the children are young and a tree or two could be establishing themselves; the sandpit might later become a pool or flower-bed. One such design is shown here (*left*).

In a very small plot, the rest of the garden may still be subjected to ball games, although in the longer plot such games could be confined to the far end where the climbing frame and a bigger swing could be placed. If one is fortunate enough to have a mature tree on the site, it may lend itself to the building of a tree-house or a rope slung over a bough with an old tyre to make a swing.

Nowhere in any garden where there are small children should there be a pool, however shallow, unless it is securely fenced in. Water has a fascination for the young and a small child can drown in as little as 15cm (6in).

The Garden of Colour

Lastly, there is the gardener who puts all his or her faith in colour, to whom, in fact, the words 'garden' and 'flower-beds' are synonymous.

You will know many a little road-side garden which you stop to admire, a billowing mass of aubrietas and bulbs, or ablaze with summer bedding: undeniably beautiful, but out of their season scarcely meriting a second glance for the simple reason that when the colour has gone there is no compensation of form. The garden is comparatively flat, a mere carpet of colour with little vertical dimension.

Outdoor Living Space

These different ideas on what a garden should be are each right, up to a point, though none goes far enough. We need a conception which is sufficiently comprehensive to embrace them all and the one which will be of the greatest assistance is that of 'Outdoor Living Space'.

Arriving at a definition will not design the garden, but it gives us a better view of our target, and with the idea of living space in mind the 'Outdoors' will be designed and developed with the same care and with the application of broadly the same principles as are used indoors.

Just as we collect and arrange the best furnishings we can afford inside the house, so our favourite plants will be disposed to the best advantage of the garden as a setting for the house. Recreation and relaxation, being essential parts of living, are also taken care of, and our varying individual needs for colour in curtains and car-

Orchard Cottage: a practical
and artistic siting of the
vegetable plot integral with
the rest of the garden.

Holebird: a rock garden for
an alpine plant enthusiast.

Yew Tree Cottage: creating three-dimensional space outdoors (iris 'Jane Phillips'; rose 'Mme Grégoire Staechelin').

Newly planted shrubs, carefully chosen for contrast and positioned to allow room to grow.

pets will find satisfaction in massed flowers outside.

Whatever aim seems to each of us the most important, the garden becomes part of the home, and, like the house, will reflect the personality of the person creating it, for our organized living space is being extended outdoors.

Once we 'live' in the garden, we need more than a patterned carpet, colourful though this may be. Our 'furniture' must be plants with bulk and form. Trees will provide height to create the impression of a ceiling and in time we engender the feeling of being within an outdoor room.

Forming a mental picture in three dimensions calls for imagination because our small shrubs and trees may grow so big that careless positioning may make them a nuisance. If arranged with foresight they will give us not a garden which is a mere pattern of colour, nor something to be viewed from a particular point at a particular time, but structure of pleasing form to grace our living space, to divide it, and at the same time to provide the enclosure and privacy which are so essential.

James Rose, the American landscape architect, in his book *Creative Gardens* defines a garden in a way which will help to form a realistic conception:

I have found it helpful to think of a garden as sculpture. Not sculpture in the ordinary sense of an object to be viewed. But sculpture that is large enough and perforated enough to walk through. And open enough to present no barrier to movement, and broken enough to guide the experience which is essentially a communion with the sky.

THE TIME FACTOR

Gardening, like any occupation which deals with nature and the land, calls for optimism and patience, without which one would never plant anything. Yet what appears to worry so many would-be gardeners is the time factor. Is it worth trying to make a garden when one is not settled? Or, if of advancing years, will one ever live to see the result of one's efforts and expense? This is a bogey which must be laid at once, though given some thought.

I know a little garden taken over by a tenant on a one-year agreement. It was dug and weathered in the winter, forked and levelled in the spring, and, at the cost of only a few pounds, looked a picture by mid-summer. A small, well-shaped lawn was laid, height was provided by sun-flowers and tobacco plants. The beds were a riot of colour from packets of seed: nasturtiums, clarkia, godetia, calendula, stocks and a few bedding plants bought at the local market. Admittedly, this garden relied almost entirely on colour; but the cost was low. Among the other plants, small shrubs were planted as an insurance against a longer stay, and by the second year they were beginning to provide form.

Making a garden is a progressive business. One does not do the work and then have to wait for several years to see results. Naturally, if we are to rely on trees and shrubs to provide form and enclosure, and the division of space, unless we are extravagant, small plants are purchased and must be given time to develop to serve their purpose to the full. There is, however, a great deal of pleasure in watching these plants grow and in the temporary filling which one will appreciate in the meantime.

The answer to the question, 'How long will it take for shrubs to grow?' must necessarily be vague. They will mature at different rates according to the particular shrub, climate, soil, and environment, so that one rarely reaches a point when it is possible to say 'This garden is now fully developed'. During the first year after planting, a tree or shrub will establish itself, and in many cases will not put on a lot of growth, often failing to flower, to the disappointment of the purchaser but to the ultimate benefit of the shrub. During the next year it will make surprising progress, particularly in a wet summer. In the third season a great many, such as diervilla, deutzia, potentilla and spiraea, will be as big as you want them, while others like lilac, magnolia, sweet bay, and maple will still be far from the required size. One can therefore plant shrubs with confidence though with some limitation of expense if one's tenancy of a house is less than three years. Trees, especially if required for screening, will take as long as 5–7 years to make a serviceable head.

It is best to select and place the really permanent shrubs and trees so that when developed they will have enough room, and to fill in with cheaper, faster growers, which can be regarded as expendable. This avoids the too-close planting of the slower plants and the inevitable problem of wastage when they begin to crowd each other.

It should be remembered that many plants which one can buy, such as roses and herbaceous plants, give excellent results during the first season and are good value for money.

Time for Planting and other Operations

Time is a recurrent factor in a programme of work. There are ideal periods for carrying out certain essential operations, but fortunately some of them can be stretched a little, as long as one realizes the calculated risk involved. One cannot always take over a new property at a moment which is right for everything, and it is sometimes necessary to do work out of its normal place in the programme in order to 'catch the season'.

Digging and cleaning the ground is best done in the autumn, and with clay it is essential to turn the soil roughly so that winter frosts can break up the clods. One misses this natural aid and the work is more difficult if delayed beyond January. On lighter land, ground preparation can go on into the spring, and levelling can continue throughout the summer provided the land does not bake too hard.

The turfing of grass areas is done in the autumn and in open weather through to the early spring, but once grass starts to grow and the weather becomes warmer, turves cannot be cut, or, if laid, will demand constant watering.

Seeding, on the other hand, is best carried out in early September while the land is still warm and rain can be relied upon. As the year advances the nights grow colder, germination is slowed down, and seeding is inadvisable after early October. If the September period is missed, the next best is early April, although there is greater competition from weeds and the risk of a hot, dry May scorching the young plants before the roots are deep enough.

Because the ideal times for planting are October for evergreens and November for deciduous plants, there is a tendency for some people to panic if the work is not done then. But, excluding the period of mid-winter hard weather, planting can go on until early March (April and May for evergreens), although with light land in dry parts of the country there is a danger from spring drought.

One must not forget the spring bulbs, wallflowers, and forget-me-nots which go in during the last months of the year and the summer bedding-out in May or the seed-sowing both of annual flowers and vegetables in the spring.

With the season dictating so much, first thought in any programme must be of planting, for the simple reason that at least some of the plants can be establishing themselves while the rest of the work goes on. This is particularly important in the case of trees for screening.

The construction of paths, walls, steps, and paved areas are all jobs which do not depend on the season

Right: It is possible to get a colourful display quickly by using bedding plants, annuals and plants in pots: *Lobelia*, *Lavatera trimestris* (annual mallow) and fuchsias in a London garden.

Below: This garden had been planted four months when the photograph was taken.

and are probably more conveniently done in the long summer evenings. Concrete work or other operations involving the use of cement should not, of course, be done during frosty weather.

THE COST FACTOR

Cost must be coupled with ownership and the time factor. An *owner* of property can spend money over a period for his own enjoyment in the knowledge that whatever he does will improve the value of his property; there are in fact many cases where a house has sold more easily because of its garden. In such cases, once a scheme has been devised, it can be developed over a long period by anyone reasonably expecting to be settled.

A *tenant*, on the other hand, is putting money into his landlord's property, and it is obviously unwise to do this to any great extent, particularly if he is liable to move. He can, however, plant quick-growing trees and shrubs in limited quantity, and make use of odd herbaceous plants given by friends, plus annuals.

At this stage cost can be discussed only in broad and relative terms, for until a design is drawn out nothing can be measured and priced; but assuming that the owner's efforts represent the labour costs, one can at least find out which items must be 'played down' if the garden is not to be extravagant.

Excluding labour, therefore, and looking at cost in terms of purchases to be made, the cheapest treatments would be to leave the land covered entirely with cheap rough grass,

which is hacked down at intervals, or to dig all over and merely keep it clean. This is obviously going to extremes. The former does not make a garden, though it approaches one when trees and shrubs are added; the latter is the basis of a vegetable garden, which must be the cheapest layout because, although there is a certain outlay, it is one which is returned with interest.

To go a step further, the rough grass could be replaced by top quality seed, or by turf at about three times the price, but with no better eventual result. This must be an economical basis to start with. Reshaping and levelling only involves labour and does not increase cash outlay, since differences in level can be accommodated by banks if necessary. Paths will be added as needed, and can vary in cost. Except on sites that are almost flat, a certain amount of walling may be preferred to retain differences in level, and some form of paving stone will be required for permanent paths, sitting areas, and the making of steps.

Left: Yew Tree Cottage: herbaceous border with delphiniums, phlox, etc., and turf path.

Below: Burnside: in this garden, the apple tree establishes the level of the shallow terrace.

The main structural material will be plants for screening, for the division of space, and the provision of form and colour. Notes on the approximate cost of such essentials can only be misleading at a time when prices rise every season, but a few good nursery catalogues will be a help in assessing the possible commitment for any scheme.

A PRACTICAL START

Of the many ways in which a garden can come into being, the one to avoid is the haphazard development that is inevitable when the project has not been given sufficient thought. Admittedly many gardens have been made without a plan, but it is a risky venture. It takes an experienced eye to size up a piece of land, divide it, and shape its parts so that there is good proportion and harmony between them.

Caution is the best approach: decide nothing until the whole has been examined on paper. Scribbles on an old envelope have their place in the early groping for ideas – works of art have been born that way – but, as the design has eventually to be transferred to the ground, it is essential to have a measured plan of the plot drawn to scale. This takes time and trouble, but since it is for the sake of a garden you may live with for years, it is worth it. The quality of the draughtsmanship does not matter, as long as you understand it yourself.

Measuring the Plot

Let us look at the most widespread of sites, the suburban plot, usually straight-sided, of variable length, with a frontage of about 12–18m (40–60ft). On the agent's plan the dimensions are usually written in, but one cannot assume that the angles at the corners are square or that the sides are parallel. We must therefore establish the angles at the corners and the relationship of the sides.

If the boundaries of the site are not already clearly defined by fences, they should be marked either by a tight length of twine at ground level where the fence will run, or a series of canes, sighted from one end so that they represent the proposed fence. The corners, particularly, should be marked by easily visible pegs or canes at the intersections of the boundary lines.

Measuring the lengths of the four sides is a straightforward matter requiring only the accuracy which comes with care, and the relationship of sides and ends is established by diagonal tie measurements across the angles. Kinks and irregularities in the fence lines are also fixed by such mea-

The plan of the site is built up by splitting the area into triangles. This is usually the first stage for drawing an outline plan to fix the relationship of sides and ends. The dark area represents the house.

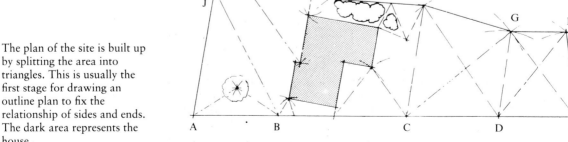

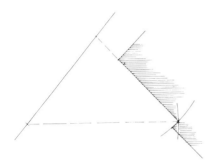

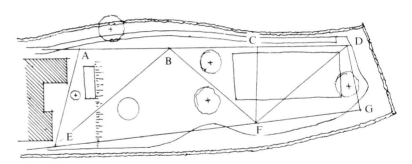

surements which really split the site up into triangles.

The position of the house, if already built or started, must be fixed, and though it may well be square with one boundary, it is unwise to take this for granted.

Quite often the line of one face of the building can be sighted to strike a side fence and its direction fixed by triangulation. These measurements (*below, left and above, left*) should be sufficient to plot the shape of a small site.

More Complicated Sites

Not every site has one long, straight, uncluttered boundary fence. Yours may be curved or kinked, or it may be impossible to see it, much less stretch a tape along it. Your plot may be an existing garden containing paths, trees, and other features and they must be put into your plan. For this we still keep to the principle of triangulation, but we set up a framework of triangles *within* the plot, and in turn measure from the lines forming the sides of these triangles to the objects being surveyed (*above, right*).

In practice there are few sites where it is impossible to sight a series of canes in a long straight line, with, on wider sites, another line roughly parallel some distance away. These two basic lines (A, B, C, D and E, F, G) can be connected by cross measure-

ments which link them accurately, and divide the intervening space into triangles.

As each of these lines is measured, the tape being used is laid taut on the ground. Details, such as trees or odd points on a fence or path, are fixed by noting distances along the line and square off it.

On a site only 9–12m (30–40ft) wide, it is often possible to lay a single line running the full length, roughly down the middle, and to tie all the detail and the boundary lines to this.

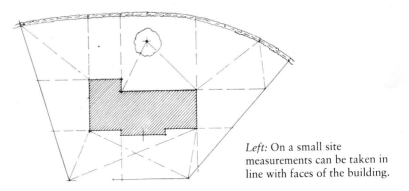

There is a somewhat unorthodox but effective method of measuring (*above*), which can be used when the building itself occupies a high proportion of the site: in other words, when the garden is relatively small. This is to start with a plan of the house and merely extend its lines, by sighting, until they strike the boundaries, at

Above, left: A long face of the house can be sighted onto a side fence. Measurements along the fence and diagonally back to the house will fix it.

Above, right: A plot of irregular outline broken up into triangles for the purpose of fixing detail.

Left: On a small site measurements can be taken in line with faces of the building.

distances which are recorded. A number of such measurements from corners and projections on the building will establish a series of points to be joined up, and tie measurements can be taken across to corners or breaks as a check in locating their exact positions.

Levels

So far our measurements have been confined to two dimensions in roughly the same plane. We have no data concerning the third dimension, the rise and fall of levels. It is obviously impracticable for the average householder to produce the necessary instruments to take levels, though they might be hired or even borrowed. A student architect or surveyor might help but, if all else fails, a spirit level and long straight edge can be used. This is a slow but certain method of ascertaining the rise or fall of the ground and its relationship to the damp-proof course of the house, so long as it is carefully carried out.

The Survey Plan

The information gathered on site must be drawn out to scale on either plain or graph paper. The latter is readily obtainable in a variety of markings, but use one which allows your plan to be of reasonable size – say a sheet approximately 75 × 50cm (30 × 20in). The compass point should be noted as well as any other relevant details, such as the presence of nearby trees or buildings which shade the plot.

This drawing will be the basic plan on which any proposed layout is built and you will soon appreciate its value. Apart from being able to judge the possibilities or limitations of its dimensions, you will see your plot from a new angle, a bird's eye view, and this in itself prompts ideas which can be tried out with ease on tracing paper fixed over the survey.

GENERAL PRINCIPLES

Design in the garden is not achieved by the rigid application of rules. It is free and creative, and will call for the controlled use of the imagination. It demands the same qualities as are found in a work of art, and we must at once search out certain principles which will be a guide not only in the conception of the garden as a whole, but in the component parts down to the placing of the smallest plant. Such principles applied to our particular medium may very well include the following:

Proportion and Scale

This might be defined as a pleasing relationship between the three dimensions – length, breadth and height. Make your lawn not too long, not too wide, perhaps containing a bed which is not overwhelmingly bulky, yet not 'lost' in its surroundings. Use materials and plants in scale with the size of your plot: for a group of trees on a *small* lawn use laburnums not limes; for a small house avoid designing a terrace or forecourt with dimensions more suited to a mansion.

Balance

This can be achieved by the careful distribution of accents over an area without necessarily spacing them equally each side of an axis. The lop-sided effect of a garden, with all the weight in one part, can be an irritation.

The curving, low wall and steps forming the boundary of the lawn provide elegance of line.

A formal pool is the focal point in this garden.

A design for a simple garden for a semi-detached house including lawn, shrub and herbaceous borders and a small pool. There is space for a vegetable patch at the end.

Unity

The component parts – lawn, borders, paved areas and separate small enclosures such as a rose garden – will each be a pleasing feature, but they must be sited and shaped so that they fit together as surely as a jigsaw to form an equally pleasing whole.

Elegance of Line and Shape

It is as easy to maintain a good shape as a bad one, and an effort should be make to design lines which are pleasing, curves without jags, which flow and carry the eye from one part of the garden to another.

Contrast and Harmony

There is great scope in the bringing together of shapes which enhance each other, curves flowing harmoniously together or by contrast, straight with curve. In the planting of the garden there are endless opportunities

Left and below: Two houses of similar character, but on a different scale: the gardens are in proportion.

for experiment which will lead to originality. The contrast of fine foliage with coarser, rounded outlines with vertical or spiked growth, the harmony of blended flower and foliage colours, and the sharp contrast of white flowers against red, yellow against purple are examples.

Focal Point

A small garden will always be dominated by the house, and rightly so; nevertheless, just as a good photograph needs a point of interest, so will the garden. This focal point will be related to the house as, for instance, on the centre line of a window or door, so strengthening the bond between house and garden. It can be some inert object such as an ornament, pool, seat or summerhouse or it can be a group of trees or other plants, and though there may be other accents they will not detract from the main one. This focus of attention is necessary in other parts of larger gardens lying well away from the house, especially in the creation of separate little units.

Formal or Informal

One of the first decisions to be made is whether or not to be strictly formal throughout or, if you dislike the rigi-

In larger gardens, it is often
necessary to provide a focal
point by creating a garden
within the garden.

Chidmere: in this formal
garden, with clipped hedges
and yews, the eye is carried
on to the white ornament at
the end of the lawn.

A formal, 'architectural' garden with rectangular pool and tall cypresses providing strong vertical accents.

dity of straight lines, just how much freedom the site will allow for flowing lines. You may very well finish with a combination of both.

Since a geometric layout on a slope can appear to be sliding down hill, it will demand a certain amount of levelling; but this can often be done in a series of shallow terraces. A formal scheme can be restful and, properly executed, is never as severe as it appears on paper, which does not show the third dimension. For instance, a straight border, with a 45cm (18in) strip of paving stone laid along its front edge, is indicated on the plan by three straight lines. It looks hard, but visualize it as a billowing mass of foliage and colour, lifted here and there by a small tree or shrub, with foreground plants spilling freely on to the stone, and the impression is altered.

The formal garden is honest. There is no need to disguise its size, or that of the plot in which it is set; the hedges, fences or walls, which define its well-proportioned shape, take up very little of the precious space and are clearly visible.

Informality, on the other hand, will rely for its effect on the masking of as many of the surrounding hard lines as possible, an effect best achieved by planting in depth. This is the use of shrubs and trees of ascending height, planted in groups one behind the other, with the most satisfying results; but it takes space and, for this reason, on a narrow site, is most easily contrived if the planting can run across the plot, or on one side only.

Whatever lines you choose, there is one seemingly small point to watch as you develop your plan. If you want to preserve a sense of space, keep the middle open. An odd specimen shrub or a group of small trees can be intriguing accents, and give perspective to your garden, but to fill the centre with a pattern of beds is like placing a large table in the centre of a small room: it immediately reduces the apparent size and prohibits free circulation.

Designing for the Style of the House

Designing to suit the style of the house, to those with houses of a definite period, is of course desirable, but

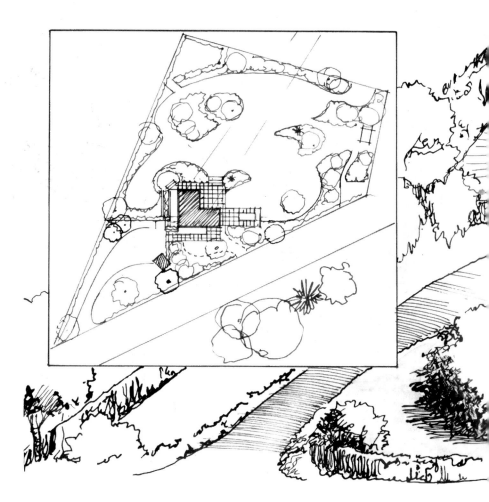

Linleys: Plan and sketch for an informal garden, although with some formality near the house.

The Willows: to preserve a
sense of space, keep the
middle of the garden open.

affectation must be avoided, and too
purist an attitude will result in your
being bogged down and afraid to
move. A history of gardening through
the ages is beyond the scope of this
book, but it is as well to remember
that gardens as originally laid out
have been altered time and again

without ill-effect. It is good design,
irrespective of period, which makes
certain antiques fit harmoniously into
a contemporary room, and vice versa,
and observance of the principles leading to good design will have equally
happy results in the garden.

2 THE DIVISION OF THE SITE

The first step is to mark off the plot in broad divisions according to use, and this is best done free-hand on tracing paper pinned over the site plan. Allocate an area for vegetables, lawn, main border, a possible line for the service path, and so on. This disposition of the main component parts of the garden – your own requirements – is straightforward, but important because you are now setting up the framework of your scheme. You will be influenced to a great extent by practical considerations: for example, any enclosure for small children or a utility area for drying linen will be close to the kitchen; the service path must be functional but kept to a minimum.

have to be deeply dug, cleaned and kept clean, and it is wise to mark off an area and consider what this will entail.

Fruit may well be included in the kitchen garden, but though vegetables and fruit trees can be grown together while the latter are young, this is not a satisfactory arrangement as a long-term policy. In the small garden, therefore, the inclusion of standard, half standard, or bush trees means the loss of the ground under their spread as far as production is concerned.

Fruit trees are offered by nurserymen usually in the following forms: standard, half standard, bush, pyramid, cordon, espalier and fan-trained. Cordons, espaliers and fan-trained trees take up least space; cordons and

The Willows: vegetable garden.

THE COMPONENT PARTS

Vegetable Garden

Vegetables straight from the garden, with the natural bloom still on them and handled only by yourself, have an indescribable freshness which makes them well worth the time and effort. Since the area of land required for growing them may be a fairly high proportion of the whole, the vegetable garden must be considered first.

Deciding how much to grow will depend on your own inclinations, the size of the family and the area of ground you can manage. It will all

Forms of fruit trees available.

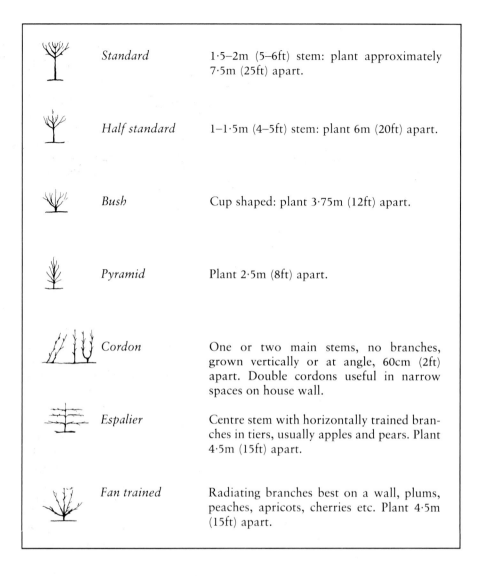

	Standard	1·5–2m (5–6ft) stem: plant approximately 7·5m (25ft) apart.
	Half standard	1–1·5m (4–5ft) stem: plant 6m (20ft) apart.
	Bush	Cup shaped: plant 3·75m (12ft) apart.
	Pyramid	Plant 2·5m (8ft) apart.
	Cordon	One or two main stems, no branches, grown vertically or at angle, 60cm (2ft) apart. Double cordons useful in narrow spaces on house wall.
	Espalier	Centre stem with horizontally trained branches in tiers, usually apples and pears. Plant 4·5m (15ft) apart.
	Fan trained	Radiating branches best on a wall, plums, peaches, apricots, cherries etc. Plant 4·5m (15ft) apart.

espaliers can be grown supported by wire beside a path. Pyramids and bush are most suitable for growing in a group in the vegetable garden.

Soft fruit such as red, black and white currants and gooseberries are best in a block planted 1·5m (5ft) apart, in rows also 1·5m (5ft) apart, though gooseberries lend themselves to training as cordons and can even be made into a hedge. Raspberries should be in rows 1–1·5m (4–5ft) apart with plants 30cm (1ft) apart in the row. Strawberries, planted at intervals of 45cm (18in) in rows 75cm (2ft 6in) apart and sited near other soft fruit, can be included in a wire cage enclosing the lot to give protection against birds.

The most suitable place for the siting and incorporation of the vegetable garden, although not necessarily ideal from the working point of view, but with regard to the scheme as a whole,

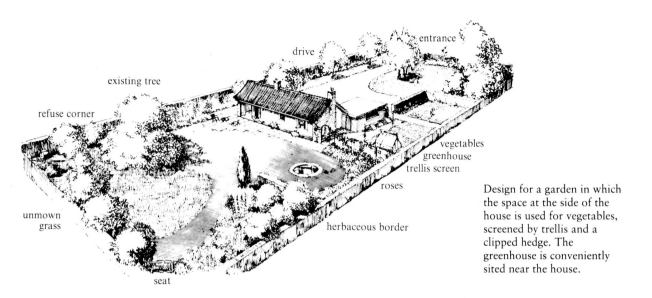

drive · entrance

existing tree

refuse corner

unmown grass

seat

vegetables
greenhouse
trellis screen

roses

herbaceous border

Design for a garden in which the space at the side of the house is used for vegetables, screened by trellis and a clipped hedge. The greenhouse is conveniently sited near the house.

is right across the far end of the plot.

The position must be open to sunlight, away from the drip and shade of trees, preferably with a gentle south-facing slope, and with protection from strong winds. If the shelter does not already exist, it must be provided. The plot should be reached by a clean, firm path which can be continued down the vegetable garden; the path should avoid the centre line of the narrow plot, or the rows of vegetables flanking it will be too short. Within the garden, hard paths should be kept to a workable minimum to avoid interference with a machine cultivator.

Obviously if the end of the plot is unsuitable, the whole vegetable area must be drawn into a satisfactory siting, possibly at the expense of the remainder of the layout. It is a matter of deciding which is more important. It is only on wide sites that one has much choice in the positioning, for it is only under such circumstances that one should ever consider biting away any of the width from a strip of land already too narrow.

For those fortunate enough to have wide plots, beside the house is a good place for vegetables. If the building is not equidistant from each side fence, there will often be sufficient room for a small salad and herb garden.

Allow too much rather than too little space for vegetables. Space will be needed for a compost heap, a bonfire, and possibly a tool shed, a greenhouse and frames. Site these at the end of the plot nearest to the remainder of the garden to cut down the distance for wheeling rubbish from all parts.

The Greenhouse

The designer's task in siting the greenhouse is to answer satisfactorily the questions of function, cost, type of material, maintenance and practical use as well as fitting the greenhouse harmoniously into his or her overall scheme.

There are three basic types of domestic greenhouse: warm, frost-protected and cold. The type of greenhouse will play an important part in

Abinger Mill: a greenhouse
can be an attractive feature in
the garden.

Opposite: Greenhouses: basic
shapes
1 conventional or span roof
2 Dutch lights
3 conservatory or lean-to
4 and 5 octagonal

its siting and this is a consideration to bear in mind when making your choice as well as the obvious criteria of cost and function.

Warm house
A wide range of plants can be grown in a warm greenhouse, and for vegetables a longer cropping season is possible. This must be weighed against the initial installation costs and maintenance of a permanent supply of heat (minimum winter temperature 18°C).

Frost-protected house
This provides protection from frost and will ensure that crops such as tomatoes can be planted earlier and remain longer in the house. A winter crop of lettuce would mature earlier than in a cold house and a number of tender plants, such as pelargoniums and fuchsias, can be overwintered. For a frost-protected house, a system of free blowing warm-air heating will be needed. A paraffin or Calor gas heater, *with ventilation*, would supply this (minimum winter temperature 7°C).

Cold house
To appreciate the value of a cold house, which has no artificial heat at all, one has only to imagine the shelter for the gardener and plants when there is a howling gale, torrents of rain or sleet, or a blanket of snow. In the cold house are grown plants which would grow out of doors, but with the protection of glass will mature earlier. Plants such as chrysanthemums are protected in October and November to enable them to give better quality blooms. The raising of young vegetable plants is assisted.

Siting the Greenhouse
Greenhouse specialists consider that an east-west ridge is best, but are prepared to admit that if conditions do not allow this any other orientation is admissible. It should be sited in full sun, avoiding the shadow of tall buildings or trees. It should not be placed on low ground which could be a frost pocket, nor in a windswept position. The entrance should be at the end away from the prevailing wind.

For a warm greenhouse heated by electricity or gas, it is essential to site it near the mains supply. The laying on of electricity is best left to specialists, who will know the irksome regulations designed to prevent you at some future date stabbing in a fork and electrocuting yourself. Installation of either gas or electricity will have to be checked by the appropriate board if laid by other than their own workmen. The fact that the frost-protected house can be kept above zero in winter by portable means gives greater latitude in the siting of this type of greenhouse. A cold house could even stand on concrete or in an open backyard.

In siting your greenhouse, you should also bear in mind its proximity to the water supply, whether waterbutt or outside tap. Carrying water to a distant greenhouse can be a tedious business.

Shape
The traditional greenhouse has vertical sides and a ridged roof. A variation is the type known as Dutch Lights, where the sides are made from large panes of glass, with a slight cant inwards. For very small gardens, there is an octagonal greenhouse which requires the minimum amount of space and is so pleasing a shape that it could form a feature in any garden design. Finally, there is the 'lean-to' greenhouse, which should be built against a south-facing wall; if placed against a wall containing a door into the house, it could be turned into a conservatory.

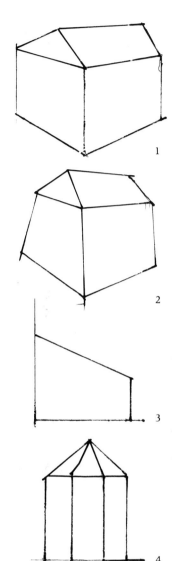

1

2

3

4

5

Materials

Greenhouses constructed of white-painted timber need maintenance every two years or so; those made of Western Red Cedar – a beautiful wood – also need preservative at intervals, although easier to handle than paint. Aluminium alloy houses, with members so delicate that they keep out very little light, are more expensive but require very little maintenance.

Siting a greenhouse near the house has much to commend it. It allows the owner of a cold house to add a little or a lot of warmth at a later date by using electricity. The conservatory built on the south wall can use heat supplied by a pipe through the wall, from the central heating system. A free-standing house near the back door is also convenient for the owner.

The Service Path

The most difficult of sites, the long narrow strip of land, has its own particular problem not encountered in larger gardens. It is the preservation of the already meagre width, the creation of a sense of space, and, when possible, the illusion that there is more than actually exists. In such cases the line of the service path plays an important part.

In a long, narrow room, one would not start to furnish by running a long, narrow carpet down the centre, unless wanting to emphasize the length. It is more usual to break the length with lines across, or to use an all-over carpet. So in the narrow garden, the fewer strong lines and shapes running down the site the better.

The four diagrams (*below*) illustrate this principle. In A the plot is split into two useless halves by a centre path; the narrowing can be felt at once. This arrangement is all too common and tempts one to develop along this line with strip beds, standard roses, wooden pergolas or arches, which accentuate the fault, since there are now not only long shapes on plan, but strong, vertical accents along the centre line. The panels each side of the path become unmanageable strips of grass, too small to be a lawn, difficult to mow and edge – and the width has gone. In B the same path has been moved to one side – note the improved feeling of space. (The path should be on the side with least sun, leaving the other for a border.) In C and D, the path crosses from one side to the other. There is no loss of space; in fact, lines crossing the site tend to increase its apparent width, a point to be remembered when shaping borders within this framework.

The three gardens shown right further illustrate this point. Each is the same plot, but in A the pergola down the centre of the garden and the strip beds accentuate to an unfortunate degree the narrowness of the site. In B the path is to one side and, apart from one tree, the middle of the garden is open. The neighbouring plot (C) is the same size with the path crossing over to the shaded side.

The splitting of the plot lengthwise by tangible features such as paths and beds can be aggravated by imaginary lines leading the eye down the length. Unrelieved lines of planting following

Four layouts showing diagrammatically various positions for the service path and its effect on a small, rectangular plot.

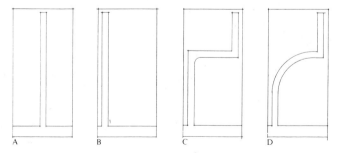

A   B   C   D

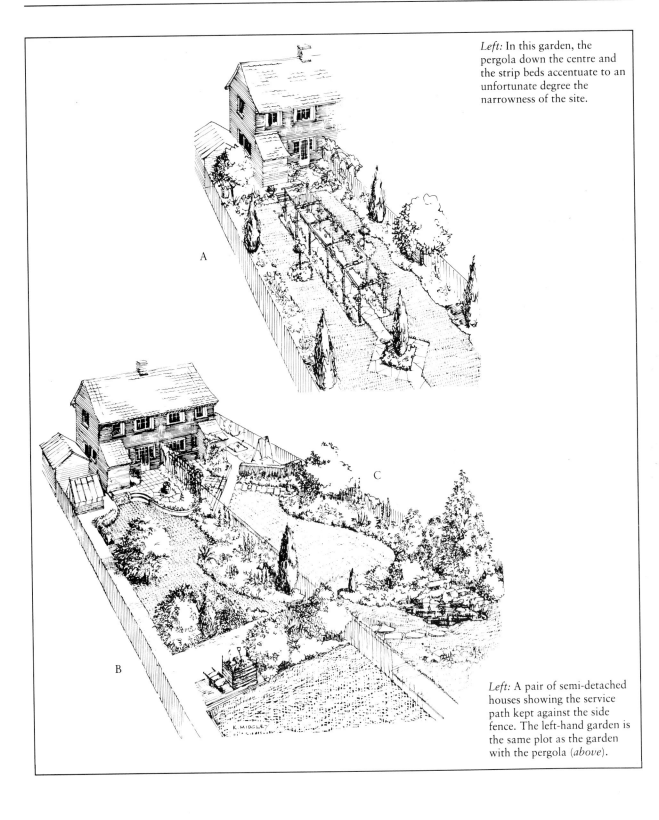

Left: In this garden, the pergola down the centre and the strip beds accentuate to an unfortunate degree the narrowness of the site.

Left: A pair of semi-detached houses showing the service path kept against the side fence. The left-hand garden is the same plot as the garden with the pergola (*above*).

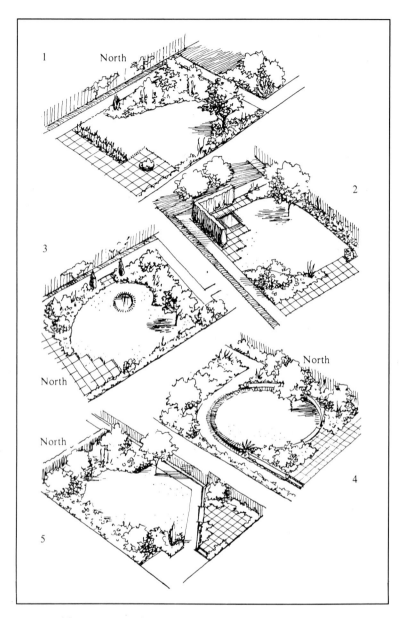

Five possible treatments of a
small back garden where the
service path crosses the plot.

the boundary fences will do this, and
should be avoided in a narrow plot.

The service path is a strongly
marked feature in a small plot and can
dictate the treatment of the area it cuts
as it crosses over. The five sketches
(*left*) show different ways in which
this basic structural line can be
developed:

1 A simple arrangement of free
lines, the main planting facing south.
The balance is maintained by a tree on
the south side, and an extension to the
terrace opposite the living-room windows, but the border along this fence
faces north and is narrow. A group of
shrubs at the head of the vegetable
garden gives interest and acts as a
screen.

2 This assumes a fairly flat site
which would allow a small formal
pool or bed in the angle of the path; it
is backed by a clipped hedge with fruit
trees behind, and the weight of the
feature balanced by a tree, and a shrub
group on the other side.

3 A flat site facing south. There is
no terrace, but the paved sitting-out
area is shaped in a simple manner, to
turn into the plot, the sharp stepped
edge of the paving contrasting with
the boldly curved border. For want of
space the border on the west side is
narrow but given weight by tree
planting.

4 A formal arrangement for a site
with a little slope; the change in level is
accommodated by a long continuous
step along the edge of the lawn, or by a
low wall in the same position.

5 Using a terrace built on an
oblique line (though equally adaptable to a flat site), the path crosses the
site under the terrace wall, and the
whole garden is built on the new angle
so established. Building a design on a
diagonal line is further developed on
page 52.

Utility Area

Unless a small yard has been incorporated in the building layout, an area conveniently near to the kitchen should be considered for domestic activities such as the drying of linen, the extra fuel bunker, dustbins and so on. This may be screened from the road by the garage but, if not, vision can be blocked by a tall hedge, fence, wall, or trellis, with a similar barrier between the utility and the rest of the garden.

Such an arrangement is suggested in plot C on page 37 where, owing to lack of space, a utility area is combined with children's corner and separated from the rest of the garden by a hedge. (For further notes on screening, see page 56.)

The Body of the Garden

Having provisionally written off a section for vegetables and for utility, and with a tentative line sketched in for a service path, the remaining ground might well be referred to as the body of the garden. It is in this part that the bond between garden and house will be apparent and it should therefore be designed on lines which defer to the building. Such deference can, for example, take the form of an axial line on plan, centred on an important window or door, e.g. terrace steps, if needed, placed not in some indeterminate position but related to the building. The designs on pages 80–85 each show a terrace designed so that it becomes one unit with its particular building.

Parts of the garden farther away from the house may be shaped about an extended axial line as in the design on pages 48–9, or oblique views from a window can be created, as in the design on page 33, down the mown grass walk to the seat in the foreground of the sketch.

Making a start is half the battle. Look at the plan and mark the centre lines of the windows, then go outside, stand well away, and look back at the house. Is it so isolated that it needs support? Or is it too much a mass of brick and mortar? If so, and if you cannot plant a tree alongside, mark on your plan a possible position forward of the building. Does the house appear too tall? A terrace 15cm (6in) below damp proof course level will help, so will a tree with a tendency to the horizontal in the branching. Conversely, the lines of a long, low building will be emphasized by the contrast of fastigiate or upward-reaching trees.

Looking down the site from the main window, is there a view to be framed or something to be screened out? Mark on your plan the possible position for a tree or trees for this purpose. Trees must not be afterthoughts: they are part of the structure of the garden and can easily affect the general shaping of your plan.

A house with a symmetrical elevation will lead you to work on a similar balance in the garden, but you should not try to force this on a house which is not symmetrical. The location of the main window might even make it difficult to do so. It is quite common for this to be uncomfortably close to the boundary fence.

Axial Lines

It follows that it is sometimes a good thing to turn an axial line *into* the plot at an angle, and to do so with such emphasis and precision that the change in direction cannot be overlooked.

From a window, for instance, one tends to look out at right-angles to the window pane, and if this should take

Right: Here the line of vision
from the main window is
intentionally deflected
towards a feature on the other
side of the garden by the
shaping of the steps.

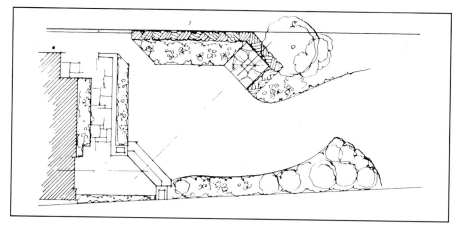

the eye to a view, all well and good;
but the line of vision can be blocked,
and the eye will then seek its own way
round the obstruction, or it can be
deflected by the shaping of some feature such as a flight of steps built at an
angle, or a formal arrangement of
planting designed to have the same
effect.

This is illustrated in the sketch
above where the need is exaggerated
by a side fence running inwards – in
fact, a tapering plot. The house might
be semi-detached or detached, but it is
likely that the living-room window
will be near the side fence. A line
square off the window runs very close
to the boards, so it is turned sharply at
the steps. We have a satisfactory link
with the house in that the steps are
placed directly opposite the main window and the terrace will later be
shaped to conform to the outline of
the building, but we have also started
in a precise and orderly manner a new
oblique movement across the plot.
This new line can be given extra emphasis by siting at its far end some
small feature such as an ornament,
a seat, or a commanding piece of
planting.

There are occasions when this
breaking away at an angle can be
employed other than when forced
upon one by the circumstances described above. It could be used as a
means of fanning out on a site which
has width but little length. A house
with a window roughly central might
have opposite the window a semi-
circular arrangement of steps leading
off at 45° on each side of the centre
line, as shown (*left*).

THE PRIORITY OF STRUCTURE

At this stage in the planning we are
concerned with the overall shaping,
and it is important not to digress and
design details which should come
later. Perhaps I might quote a personal

Below: A semi-circular
arrangement of a small
terrace with two flights of
steps leading off at 45° on
each side of the centre line.

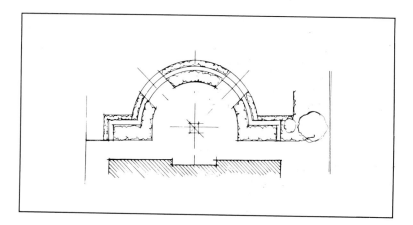

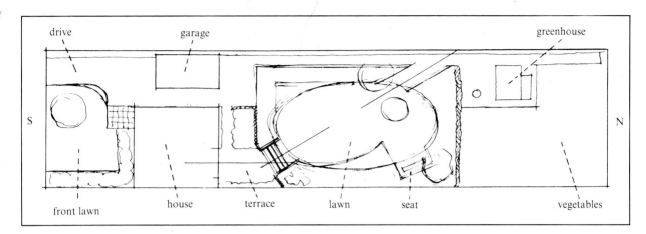

drive   garage   greenhouse

S   N

front lawn   house   terrace   lawn   seat   vegetables

experience to stress this point. Many years ago, on my second day at Art School, a number of us, all new students with little previous training, were told to make drawings of the casts of classical figures, not because we were ready for this, but so that the staff could assess any latent ability. I started to rough out the proportion on a sheet of cartridge paper with timid, faint ticks, and then fell into the trap of immediately making a careful study of the head. I received a jolt, my first lesson. I was told, kindly but firmly, that though the head mattered I was trying to finish the drawing before it had been started. In five minutes I learned that detail is not attempted until one has captured the spirit of the pose, the direction of the planes which make up the figure, the unity and balance of the composition. I have never forgotten this and found later that the principle applied just as surely to garden design. A beautifully designed flight of steps, a pool or a fine specimen plant will always be worth looking at as an individual unit but will fail unless it plays its part in the general composition.

Continue then with your rough sketch plans until you have a nicely balanced and well proportioned disposition of parts which you think will be capable of further development. When you are satisfied go on to the next stage which is to make a new drawing pinned over your sketch plan revising, modifying and giving attention to detail.

DESIGNS FOR TYPICAL SITES

Site 1

This narrow plot (*above*) measures 11·5 × 48m (38 × 160ft), runs north–south and belongs to a semi-detached house with garage. To avoid cutting up the front, the way to the garage and back door is also made to serve the front door. The vegetable garden is at the north end served by a narrow path along the west fence, since that is the shortest and most direct line from the kitchen. French doors from the living-room, a common position, close to the neighbour's fence on the east side, are too close to the boundary. The axial line is therefore turned at the terrace steps, the angle accentuated by an opening in the border on the west side. Since the house faces north the terrace will not always be sunny, and an alternative sitting area is provided in the border facing south-west. The

Site 1: rough outline plan for a small garden.

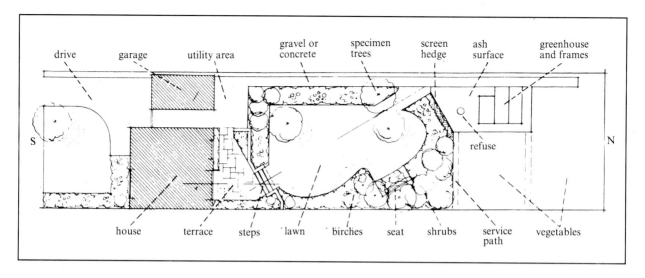

drive   garage   utility area   gravel or concrete   specimen trees   screen hedge   ash surface   greenhouse and frames

S   N

refuse

house   terrace   steps   lawn   birches   seat   shrubs   service path   vegetables

Site 1: the rough scheme developed.

greenhouse in the kitchen garden runs east–west and far enough from shrubs which screen it not to be in shadow. Refuse, compost, frames and so on are sited alongside.

The later development (*above*) indicates extra attention to aspect and at the same time an effort to maintain a pleasing shape for the lawn and a continuity of line which makes for unity.

This house has the disadvantage of facing north, but it will have the sun down the length of the garden and the best borders will therefore face the house. In the rough layout there was a groping for freedom in the shaping, but as the site is so narrow, and has this aspect, it will be best to confine free curves to the borders facing south and west making those on the other sides much more restricted in shape and size. The curves are clean and flowing without wriggles which are fussy and make mowing difficult.

Curves on a plan can be deceptive. With a small site they must necessarily swing fairly sharply, but an effort should be made not to put ripples into them. A gentle curve on paper looks more vigorous on the ground. You

will appreciate this if you draw a slightly bowed line, then hold the paper horizontal almost at eye level, which, to scale, is your point of view for a line marked on the ground.

This is a small plot and unless we steal land devoted to vegetables there is not room for separate little surprises; the main body of the garden can be kept entire, and yet sufficiently broken to create interest, by the arrangement of the planting. There are trees such as laburnum or small cherries at the end of the oblique axial line, and another group of silver birch in the spur which partially hides the seat recess, and which at the same time provides shade at midday.

Site 2

This is the same plot, but with two alterations: (*i*) the owner prefers formality and (*ii*) the plot runs east–west. The main axial line from the window goes farther than in the previous case and turns at right-angles at a point strongly marked by a simple feature. A formal semicircular garden is now devised, built on the new axial line. The borders will be in full sun. The

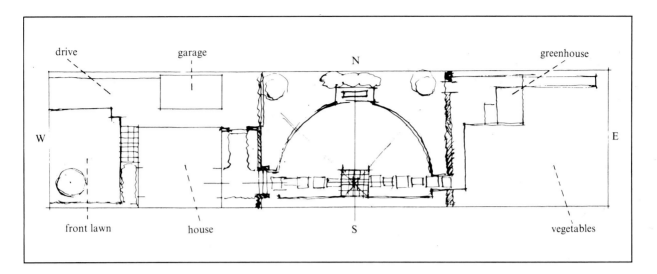

sitting-out area also faces south. The east end of the plot is the vegetable garden, as before.

The first plan shows a rough layout, the second the later development. Note that in the finalizing a service path has been included along the north fence giving a direct route to the vegetable patch. This path is on the sunny side of the plot, but it has the advantage of giving access to the back of the curved border and to any fruit which might be planted against the south-facing fence.

The area set aside for vegetables might alternatively be devoted to a small orchard, decorative and easily maintained. It will be seen that on neither site has there been any attempt to fill the middle of the garden with beds which would defeat our attempt to preserve a sense of space.

Site 2: a rough outline plan (*above*) for alternative treatment of a similar plot, but running east-west. *Below:* The rough scheme developed.

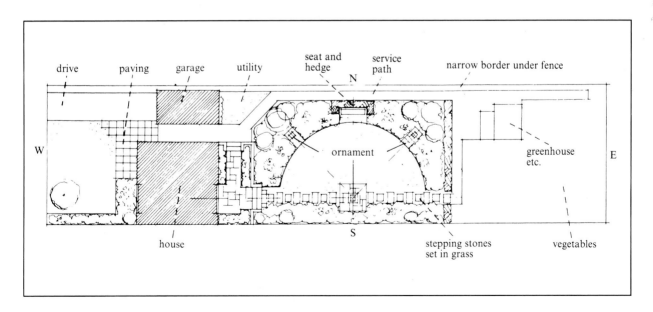

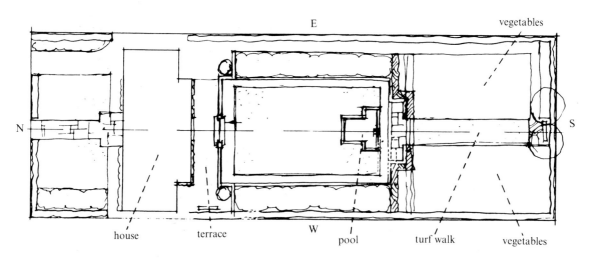

E

vegetables

N

S

house   terrace   W   pool   turf walk   vegetables

Site 3: a rough outline plan
(*above*) for a wider site.
Below: the rough scheme
developed.

Site 3

This wider site has a detached house
and a built-in garage, the whole symmetrical in conception. The garden
follows suit. Conditions of width and
symmetry enable one to work on a line
which bisects the site. For those who
like a long vista the line is even extended in the form of a wide grass
walk to a white-painted seat at the end
of the vegetable garden.

The main garden is simple and rectangular, though there is no reason
why geometric curves could not be

used. Division of the gardens is
accomplished by a formal, clipped
hedge. The utility area is at the end of
the house, and a hard service path
runs along the east fence. The front is
strictly formal but on broad lines.

The chief consideration is proportion and simplicity and the terrace
with its plain centre steps conforms to
this. Beds and borders are of practical
size to allow for their being massed
with plants which will complement
the severity of the main lines. With a
garden where proportion is so important it pays to mark out on the ground

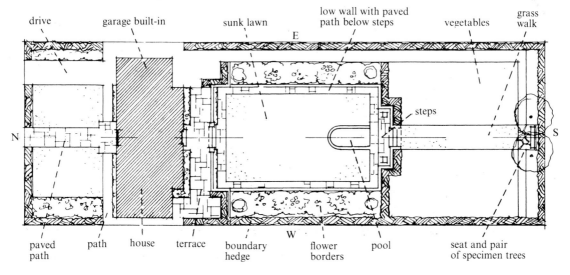

drive   garage built-in   sunk lawn   low wall with paved   vegetables   grass
                                                      path below steps   walk

E

steps

N

S

W

paved   path   house   terrace   boundary   flower   pool   seat and pair
path   hedge   borders   of specimen trees

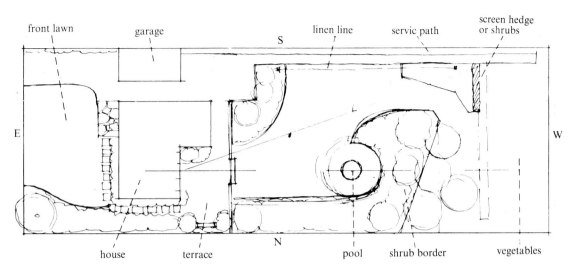

front lawn   garage   S   linen line   servic path   screen hedge or shrubs

E   W

house   terrace   N   pool   shrub border   vegetables

before finalizing the plan, since it is sometimes necessary to add a little to the length to compensate for the fore-shortening of perspective.

Levelling is called for even if the garden is on one plane, but more, of course, if the centre panel is slightly sunk, and the borders are retained by a low wall with a paved path at the foot.

The pool could be a later addition, as might the 2·5m (8ft) extension path leading to the seat.

Though considered here for a wider site, this garden might well be adapted

to a plot no more than 10·5–12m (35–40ft) wide, provided the centre line is not over-emphasized in the main garden. The centre steps could be replaced with a flight at each corner leaving the dividing hedge unbroken in the middle.

Site 4

This is the same plot running east-–west as in site 3, but with the house not centred on the site or symmetrical in design; this gives greater freedom of line in the garden. A simple, round

Site 4: a rough outline plan (*above*) for a plot similar to site 3, but with the house not centred on the site and running east-west. *Below:* the rough scheme developed.

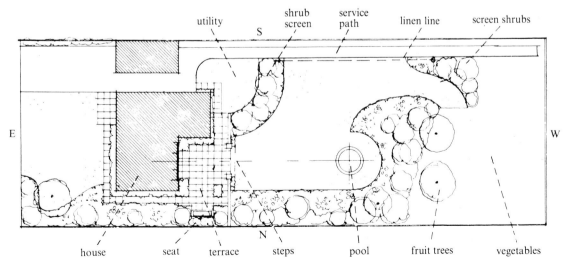

utility   shrub screen   service path   linen line   screen shrubs   S

E   W

house   seat   terrace   steps   N   pool   fruit trees   vegetables

pool on the axial line from the living-room windows is backed by a mixed border. Width of site is preserved by the lawn flowing over towards the south fence and behind the spur of border which curls round the pool. The service path is on the shaded side, with a linen line instead of a difficult border. Utility and children's space is near the garage. The terrace is sunny enough for sitting out. There is room for an orchard or vegetable plot at the west end. The front is wide open.

Note that, when the design and positioning of the house do not dictate the style so much, one has the opportunity to develop formal lines in the immediate neighbourhood of the building, blending into less rigid shapes farther away. The feeling for this in the rough design can evolve

as shown in the developed scheme. The main border, which faces south should be 3·5m (12ft) wide, or as near that as possible, in order to allow a full grouping of shrubs and flowers. This is a good site for a border; it runs away from the window so that looking down the length, seasonal gaps are not seen. It has background in the boundary hedge or boards (covered by climbers) and is in full sun. The children's garden or utility area, sited near the kitchen, is screened by shrubs and the service path, which is also on this side, is convenient for the linen line.

The backing of the border to the west of the pool might be a clipped hedge which takes little space, or shrubs and trees; indeed, where vegetables are not required these trees can form a group which is part of a small

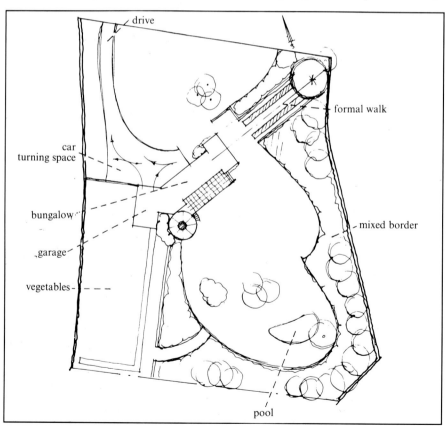

Site 5: a rough outline plan for a site of irregular outline and greater area than sites 1–4.

spinney or orchard, and be chosen accordingly.

The front is simple with a single entrance for car and pedestrians, leaving the lawn unbroken except for a specimen tree. Colour is confined to shrubs and flowers against the north fence.

Site 5

Though the majority of sites are long, narrow and roughly rectangular, no observations on garden design can be allowed to neglect the minority. There are a surprising number of sites, for obvious reasons often rural, which have width to spare.

Yours may be such a plot and we might suppose that it has on it a low,

spreading bungalow in contemporary style, sited not in relation to the road but to the sun. For the sake of argument, it needs some shelter from the east and south, possibly on account of wind or an undesirable view. In the preliminary layout space is allocated for a tree belt and the rough lines indicate a feeling for balance, in drawing attention to the west, by an increase in lawn area and tree grouping on that side.

The east end of the house contains a central window on the axis of which is hung a long rose or iris walk. The lawn flows round the house on the east side, and the site is big enough for a vegetable plot against the west boundary. This is convenient for deliveries of manure and so on; it is close to the kitchen and garage and can

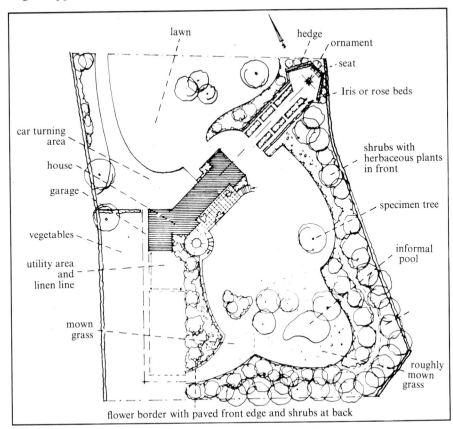

Site 5: the rough scheme developed.

contain a linen-drying ground and refuse corner. The terrace fits snugly into the recessed main south face of the building and is given a feature in the form of a circular end with a pool and shallow spiral steps. The front is wide open to the road and relies on the simplicity of lawn with tree planting, the driveway being confined to the minimum necessary for turning the car.

When the rough is later developed, attention is given to detail and the shaping of planting areas. In the interests of economy in upkeep, the south end of the lawn might be left as unmown grass, in which bulbs could be planted, with mown paths making a walk.

Site 6

This is the same plot as 5, but with different orientation and a house on traditional lines allowing a similar terrace. The main axis through the terrace steps continues through an opening in a free-flowing border to the centre of a formal rose garden. A second axial line at right-angles has a summer house or seat at one end facing the afternoon sun, and at the other a pool and weeping willow backed by a tree group. The interest here balances the weight of the planting around the rose garden. A small vegetable patch is enclosed by a hedge starting near the garage and forming a backing to a border. The

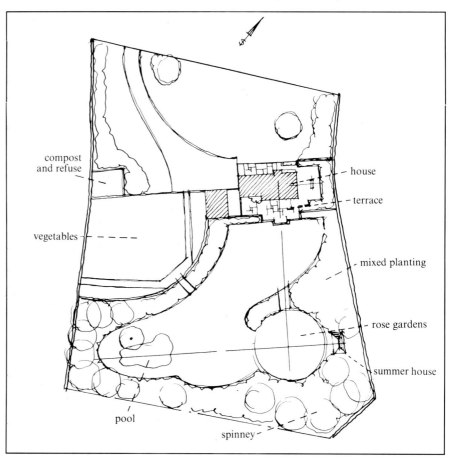

Site 6: a rough outline plan for a plot similar to site 5, but with a house built on more traditional lines and the plot with a different orientation.

rose garden, though a separate entity with its own focal point, becomes one with the remainder by the shaping of the planting areas around it and its definite relationship to the house.

In the developed plan, the areas massed in for planting on the east side of the site and along the south boundary are split by a grass or shingle walk with taller trees on the outside and shrubs on the inside. On the south the trees might well be in grass, later naturally becoming a woodland belt.

The front in this design is enclosed by a free-flowing border facing south and making a good view from the house. There are, of course, possible variations in detail: the rose garden might be enclosed by a clipped yew hedge, for example, but the scheme in general holds together, one part depending on the next, the shapes inviting movement and inspection.

This is a much bigger site than the earlier examples, one which will stand being cut up, and where there is space for separate enclosures such as the circular rose garden. There are, however, pointers for the owner of the smaller plot, which show that the same principles are at work. For example, comparison of the rough and the developed design will serve to illustrate the preservation of a sense of space. In this particular layout, the rose garden is a unit forming part of a wider scheme and the object is to create an intimate enclosed garden for

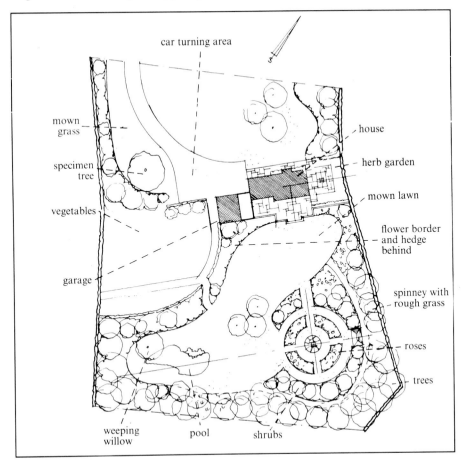

Site 6: the rough scheme developed.

growing roses in mass, not the preservation of space. But note that though the circle in the developed design is in fact slightly larger than that in the rough, the filling up of the middle makes it appear less.

Site 7

This design for a long, narrow plot is a combination of formal and informal features. The informality of the free-flowing curve of the border near the house relieves the severity of the design and gives the appearance of width, without reducing the length of the garden. From the half-way point, the division of the site lengthwise to provide a conveniently placed vegetable garden leaves only a narrow strip treated formally with twin straight borders.

Site 7: design for a long,
narrow plot that combines
formal and informal features.

Site 8

In this design, out of deference to the lines of the house, there is some imperative formality in the courtyard, but this rapidly disperses into free-flowing lines throughout the rest of the plot.

Site 8: design for a corner plot.

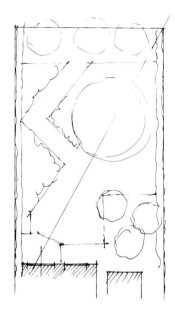

Site 9

Siting a focal point in the garden on a line square off the centre of a main window or door will secure unity between house and garden; but if for any reason it is difficult to use the centre line of a window as an axis, it is possible to build on a basic line crossing the site diagonally.

In this scheme, the house faces south-east so that the left boundary gets full sun and is obviously the place for a border; the right-hand side has little sun and must be treated accordingly. The preliminary rough (*left*) tentatively fixes a diagonal and searches for balance on this line. On the left, there is the opportunity to have a really eye-catching block of colour which is balanced by paving and three trees on the right. There is

provision for a sitting area outside the main window, but the paving under the trees could be an alternative when shade is desirable.

The finished plan shows the rough developed with substantial hedges each side of the plot; on the right-hand side, part of the hedge curls away to enclose the end of the diagonal line. This hedge might be yew or thuja, for both are dense and respond to clipping.

Near the house, the paved sitting area should be worked out in the same modules as the paving slabs in order to avoid cutting, using either 60×60cm (2×2ft) or the smaller 45×45cm (18×18in) garden slabs.

In spite of the fact that this layout is balanced on an oblique line in the first sketch, the finished plan shows one which refers to the house and sits squarely with it.

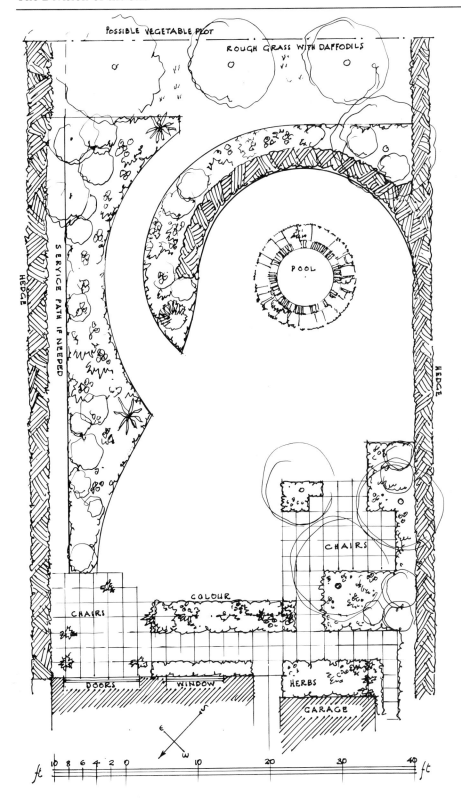

POSSIBLE VEGETABLE PLOT

ROUGH GRASS WITH DAFFODILS

HEDGE

SERVICE PATH IF NEEDED

POOL

HEDGE

CHAIRS

COLOUR

CHAIRS

DOORS   WINDOW   HERBS

GARAGE

Left: Site 9: finished plan. *Opposite:* preliminary rough (*above*) establishing balance on a diagonal line and three-dimensional sketch (*below*).

Site 10

This design for a modern plot is formal to an extreme degree; for the flat-fronted house, with its garden door almost central, calls for a formal and, indeed, a symmetrical treatment of the garden. The design could be adapted to suit sites of varying width.

The design is built on an axial line through the main door, with a second axis at right-angles halfway down the plot. The steps down from the terrace are centred on the first axial line; on the second axis hangs a pool, a seat and a backing hedge. The lawn is not really a lawn, but a carpet of grass in a frame of stone path. The formality of the design is emphasised by the four cypress trees, one at each corner.

Planned in an orderly manner without fuss, this design creates an air of stability and peace.

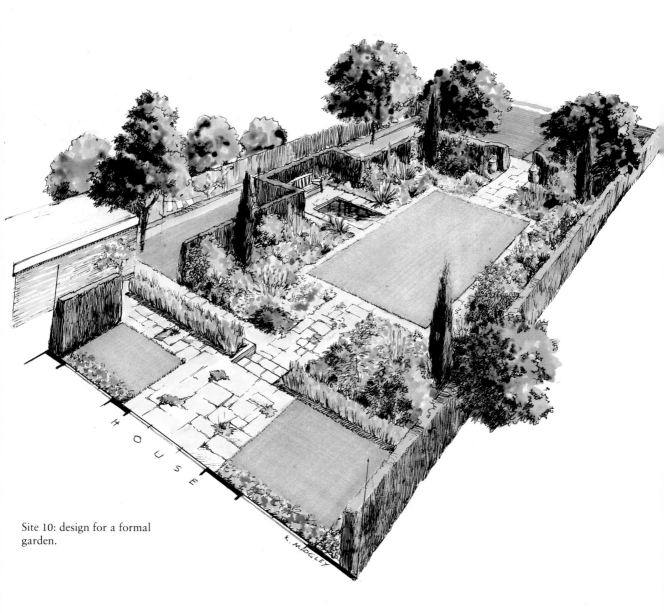

Site 10: design for a formal garden.

Site 11

This scheme for a simple, rectangular plot was designed for a garden 18m (60ft) wide, but it could be adapted for one of any dimensions within reason.

The house faces the south and the sun, with a paved terrace and sitting area outside the garden door. The pool is on the same level with three steps down to the lawn.

Another sitting out area is set within the border. At the far end of the plot, there is a small vegetable patch reached by a firm path next to the boarded fence.

In the drawing, two trees in the foreground have been 'ghosted' to avoid masking details.

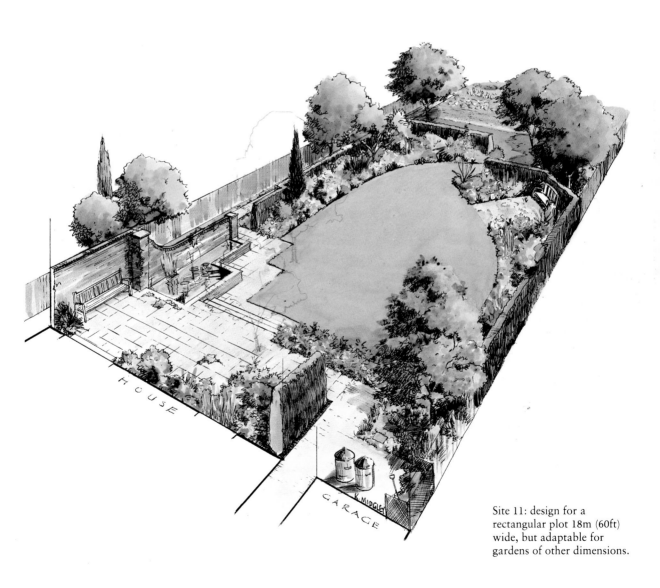

Site 11: design for a rectangular plot 18m (60ft) wide, but adaptable for gardens of other dimensions.

Opposite: Plan of two gardens in which neighbours have cooperated in staggering the dividing boundary, which can easily be rectified if ownership changes. Sketches of these two gardens are shown on page 58.

BOUNDARIES AND SPACE DIVISION

At this stage in the planning you will feel the need to devise ways of screening neighbours, without suggesting that they are unpleasant people, but because both of you like at least some part of the garden where you are not overlooked. It prevents any possibility of bad feeling with a sensitive neighbour if the matter is openly discussed as a move to your mutual advantage, with perhaps a sharing of expense and some conformity of ideas. There is little point in planning an expensive hedge if the man next door has decided to erect a wall, or a tree and shrub border if he plants different trees so close to yours that in no time they are in serious competition for head room. With a little cooperation a dividing wire fence can be 'lost' in a shrubbery built up on either side of it, with larger growers near the wire forming a background for each side. Well-chosen flowering trees could be spaced to form a ragged rather than a straight line, and arranged for attractive foliage and flower contrasts to be enjoyed by both.

Such an idea is shown here (*below*). Where the border is narrow on one side it is compensated by greater width on the other, and vice versa, while the trees are sited to avoid emphasizing the line of the division fence.

Even when the division is to be a hedge, it can be planted in a staggered line to provide a thick, dense screen (*right and overleaf*).

Plants for Hedges

Beech which keeps its brown leaf during the winter, is inexpensive. It has a reputation for being slow, but on good land, particularly in chalky districts, it will make a hedge about 1·5m (5ft) high in six years and grows to any height. The odd plant of the purple-leaf variety in the hedge is effective. Arrive at cost by allowing for plants two to the metre (yard).

Hornbeam is similar in appearance to beech; it also keeps its leaf in winter, and is more suitable on cold wet clay land. It is similar in price.

Yew is said to be the perfect hedging plant at any height. It clips well, thrives on most soils including clay and is at home on lime. It should not be used where it can be eaten by cattle as there is a poison risk. Cost using plants 45–60cm (1½–2ft) high and the same distance apart. Price per metre (yard) is 6 or 7 times that of beech.

Holly, rivalling yew for first place on moist loam, is not suitable to cold, wet soil. It is slow, but the results are worth the wait. Cost is about the same as yew.

Thuja plicata is a fine evergreen which prefers a heavy but well-drained soil; best planted small 45–60cm (1½–2ft), it withstands cutting. Rich glossy green in colour, it grows

Below: A little cooperation between neighbours in planting trees and shrubs can soon hide the dividing wire fence and the trees are so spaced that they will grow for mutual enjoyment.

division fence   lawn

pair of houses

planting   lawn

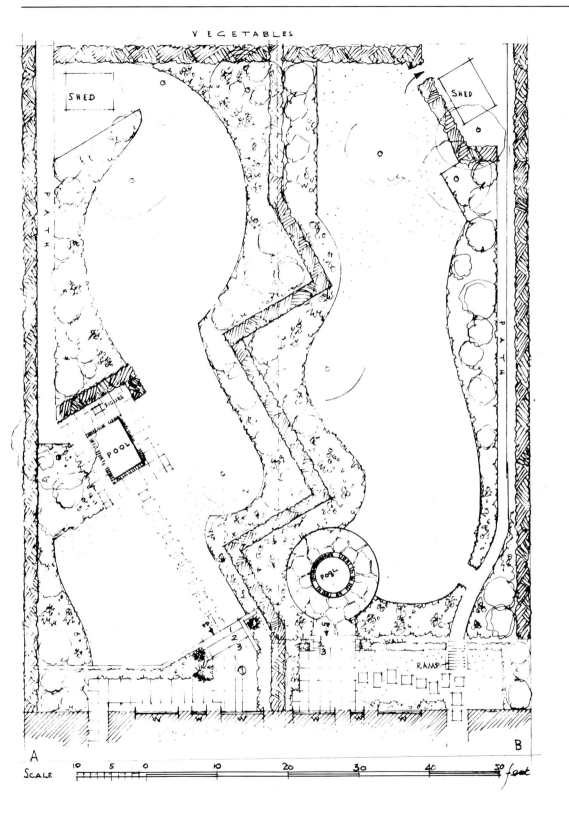

VEGETABLES

SHED

SHED

PATH

PATH

FIGURE

POOL

POOL

WALL

RAMP

A

B

SCALE

10 5 0   10   20   30   40   50 feet

Sketches of the two gardens
for which the plan is given on
page 57.

A good hedge provides a thick, dense screen. This is *Thuja plicata atrovirens*.

In this bungalow garden the yew hedge screens the road and forecourt.

to any size much faster than yew, holly, beech or hornbeam. Cost when planted 60cm (2ft) apart is approximately three times that of beech.

Lonicera nitida, sometimes called Chinese honeysuckle, is a well-known small-leafed evergreen of fast growth. It is so pliable that over 1·25m (4ft) or so in height it needs the support of wire to prevent it bending, especially under snow. It clips perfectly, but is inclined to die out at the base and has a limited life. It is best used for internal divisions; it propagates easily from cuttings. The variety 'Yunnan' is somewhat stronger. Plant 30cm (1ft) apart. Cost is variable, but this is a cheaper hedging plant than most.

Cotoneaster lacteus is a good plant for a hedge. It can be planted at 1–1·25m (3–4ft) intervals, the plants being trained towards each other. The evergreen leaf is 'white' on the underside and it has a crop of red berries which the birds leave alone. Cost, using plants from pots, due to wide spacing, is $2\frac{1}{2}$ times beech.

Cotoneaster simonsii is not really evergreen, but has a handsome berry; it is bushy, a good grower and inexpensive. Cost at 45–60cm ($1\frac{1}{2}$–2ft) high at 45cm (18in) intervals is a little more than beech.

Oval leaf Privet (not the common one which loses its leaves) has most of the virtues of a good hedge: it is inexpensive and easy to grow, making a solid wall up to 2·5m (8ft) or so. However, it is greedy and will impoverish the soil near it; some people find the rate of growth requires too frequent clipping. The golden variety is useful for a splash of highlight, particularly when seen at a distance. It is slower and more expensive. Oval leaf privet, similar in size to beech, costs fifty per cent more per metre (yard) as the plants are spaced at 30cm (1ft) intervals. For Gold multiply by three.

For a site boundary in rural areas there is a lot to be said for Myrobalan plum, which is an excellent grower, inexpensive and makes a tall hedge; it is particularly useful as a wind shield since it is dense, though not evergreen. Cost, using plants 60–90cm (2–3ft) high 45cm (18in) apart, is less per metre (yard) run than beech. The Purple Leaf Plum, *Prunus cerasifera* 'Pissardii', a red form of the above, costs about twice as much as beech per metre (yard). 'Nigra' has a dark, chocolate leaf. Either mixes well with the green.

In similar conditions *Crataegus monogyna* (quickthorn) makes a fine sturdy hedge for all time; cheap, dense but not evergreen, it calls for patience. This and privet should be pruned after planting to encourage growth from the base, which is important in the establishment of a sound framework. The cheapest of them all – 45–60cm ($1\frac{1}{2}$–2ft) at 30cm (1ft) intervals – it costs half the price of beech.

Except in temperate districts near the coast, it is better to avoid *Cupressus macrocarpa* for hedging. A handsome and exceptionally speedy grower it makes a fine tree, but it resents being cut, and is liable to die as a sizeable plant during a patch of bad winter weather. It has its uses in the garden in positions where it can be left to develop, or to serve as a temporary screen until such time as a hardier plant is big enough to take over. One of its offspring, however, which delights in the name *Cupressocyparis leylandii*, has the speed and grace of *Cupressus macrocarpa* with inherited toughness from its other parent, which makes it a good choice for a quick handsome evergreen hedge. It should, however, always be planted out of pots. The cost of 45–60cm ($1\frac{1}{2}$–2ft) plants is high at 60cm (2ft) intervals – up to three times the cost of beech.

These are a few, but there are others to be seen in nurseries, not as commonly used for the purpose, but very suitable when there is room for them to develop as flowering plants. Lilac, forsythia, philadelphus (mock orange), rose and spiraea are examples which, if allowed to grow freely, can be a magnificent sight. Laurel, *Cotoneaster* 'Cornubia' and *Berberis stenophylla* are evergreens which must be allowed plenty of room to give their best: 2·5–3·25m (8–10ft) strip for the first two and 1·5–2m (5–6ft) for the berberis.

Man-Made Fences and Screens

An alternative to a live hedge is a manufactured structure on which plants can be grown. It is best not to make this so ornamental that it attracts attention at the expense of the plant it is bearing. A simple sawn trellis is to be recommended, preferably with the wood battens vertical and horizontal which always seems less busy than the expanding diagonal kind.

Simplicity in design and some conformity to the lines of the house are important when trellis is used close to the building, the top rail, for instance, carrying the line of the garage roof or a window lintel. Finished in matching paint and draped with foliage the frame belongs to both house and garden and helps to unite them.

Rustic work has a limited use and is most suited to those parts of the garden farthest from the house. Here again simplicity in design is to be preferred to much criss-crossing of poles and over-elaborate brackets at the junction of vertical and horizontal members. For practical reasons use unpeeled larch, and not fir which is

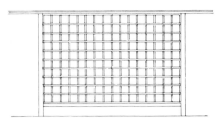

Left: A simple sawn trellis.

less durable, and make your vertical main posts in 8–10cm (3–4in) diameter timber for solidity.

While there is beauty to be found in a single piece of gnarled and twisted timber, even stripped of its bark, when a number of such lengths are nailed together to form a rough rectangle, crossed and recrossed by similar pieces, rusticity is overdone and out of place in the small garden.

Above: A trellis with climbers provides a good screen between two gardens.

Below: A rustic trellis made from unpeeled larch.

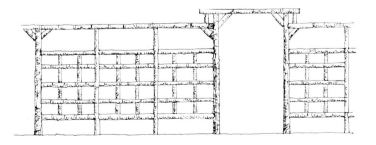

Town garden with wall and
trellis boundary screen (roses
'Zéphirine Drouhin' and
'Paul's Scarlet Climber').

A trellis screen can provide
internal division within the
garden.

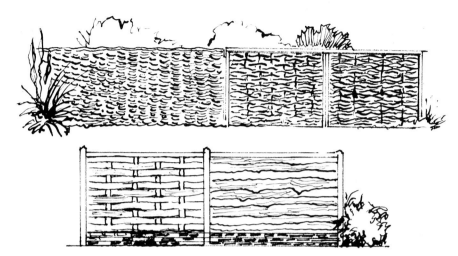

Osier-hurdle fencing.

Inter-woven fencing panels
fixed to concrete posts are
useful for a quick screen.

A well-clothed trellis is an effective wind break, but it is often necessary to use a screen of closer mesh for privacy. The widely advertised sawn slat panels fixed to wooden or concrete posts are useful, especially on the boundary. This is true of osier hurdles which are neat if set in a framing between wooden posts, though they may well be laced to thin-angle iron stakes. When close to the source of supply consider having the fence woven on site in one continuous band.

A boundary screen that is often overlooked is the combination of low fence and trained trees. Here the trees are trained so that the branches grow fanned out on each side of the main trunk; shoots which grow sideways are encouraged and those growing outwards are cut off. In time this produces a hedge on stilts, so to speak, and grown above a fence such a 'hedge' will screen out anything at a higher level. Even in the early years, when the trees are no more than say 2·5m (8ft) high, they will no doubt be doing a useful job. Growing trees in this way is called 'pleaching'; it is an old skill and a fine example using hornbeam can be seen at Hidcote in Gloucestershire.

Pleached trees adding to the
height of a pale fence. The
pales placed alternately each
side of the horizontals allow
air through.

Right: Behind the foreground trees, translucent plastic material clamped between wooden frames make admirable screens against wind and vision without blocking the light.

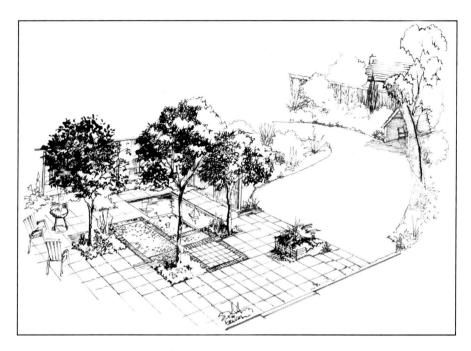

Brick wall strengthened with piers.

Sheets of flat translucent plastic material are available from builder's merchants. These clamped between two wooden frames make admirable screens against wind and vision without blocking the light. They can be used for a small enclosure within the garden, at the end of a terrace close to the house or, in the case of a tiny town garden, as a boundary division. The material is also made in corrugated sheets which can be framed to make moveable screens with obvious advantages.

For those who like to try their hand at brickwork, a 115mm (4½in) wall is thick enough if strengthened at 2–2·5m (6–8ft) intervals with whole brick or one-and-a-half brick piers. If second-hand material is used they should be bricks from external work to guard against the possibility of weather erosion.

Within the garden effective shelter can be given to a border and a pleasing space-divider made by a brick wall 1–1·25m (3–4ft) high with one-and-a-half brick piers at intervals carried up to a height of 2–2·5m (6–7ft) and carrying a timber beam along which climbers can be trained. To ensure stability it is wise to build into each pier to its full height a 15mm (½in) soft

Creating space division within the garden with (*top*) bamboo-pole frame; (*middle*) frames with nylon cord; (*below*) a single row of brick piers fronting a hedge.

Above: Trellis panel as a
boundary fence.

Right: Perforated wall made
from concrete units.

iron rod threaded at the top so that
when a drilled timber is laid on it the
whole can be secured by a washer and
nut. On the boundary the space between the piers might be filled with a
trellis panel and clothed with climbing
plants.

For the ambitious garden builder
there are some very good concrete
units which when assembled form a
perforated wall rather like a honey-
comb. Others made in blocks 30cm
(1ft) square and 10cm (4in) thick do
the same thing in a variety of patterns.
The cost varies with the design and
delivery distance.

3 LEVELLING

The very word 'levelling' conjures up a picture of hard work, and it is. Digging out soil – especially clay – barrowing, and respreading is perhaps the one operation in garden-making which can become so tedious that one regrets having started. The final result will be satisfying, but for a long time, especially for the lone worker, there seems no end to the work. For this reason alone levelling should be reduced to a minimum.

In the initial stages of the planning, the existing configuration of the ground should be allowed to give a lead to its future shaping. For instance, assuming that there is some slope and that it is running evenly away from the building, it would be sensible to think in terms of one or more simple terraces also generally parallel with the house. This arrangement would not necessarily be forced upon a site with a diagonal fall or one from side to side. In such cases the higher ground on which the house stands would probably run out along one of the side fences, and to carve this away not only makes work, but creates a wedge-shaped cutting which has to be retained by a wall (*below, b*). It would be better to level up around the building and allow at least some of the high ground along the

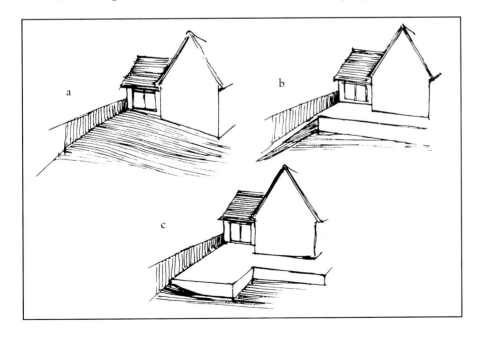

A plot with a diagonal fall diagrammatically shown where the shaping of the terrace conforms to the fall of the ground.

An L-shaped terrace with steps down is a convenient design for levelling where the ground falls away on the left-hand side.

fence to remain, forming a terrace basically L-shaped (c), page 67). This might develop as shown in the drawing (above).

There are a number of practical points to be borne in mind when designing a scheme involving levelling, the first being the height of the ground next to the house. Even with modern cavity walls it is wise to keep the earth or other surface at least two courses of brickwork or about 15cm (6in) below the damp proof course.

Except for cases in which levelled ground is to be finished with gravel, paving or some such inert material, top soil must be kept on the surface, at least 15cm (6in) of it for grass and 30cm (12in) or more for beds. This means the removal, stacking and re-placing of top soil to allow levelling of the subsoil, but in practice most of the work can be reduced to a single operation. A small section is stripped of good vegetable earth which is set aside. Subsoil is then cut away or made up to a level 15 or 30cm (6 or 12in) below the proposed new level. Top soil from the next section of the work is thrown forward on to this and consolidated. The operation is repeated section by section, the top

soil originally set aside being used to spread on the last section. In this way there is a saving in labour and the work is 'completed' as it proceeds with encouraging results.

Re-shaping of the ground should be so designed that any established tree can remain at original ground level. It will not look well standing on a pimple of raised soil, though a certain amount of mounding or hollowing is possible, especially in informal schemes. The roots should not be unearthed and it is certainly unwise to build up soil round the base of the trunk. This can cause fatal rotting of a collar of bark, vital to the well-being of the tree.

When building up ground, do not dump one barrowful on top of another, but spread in thin layers and consolidate about 15cm (6in) at a time. A roller is not the best tool for consolidating because it can span hollows and leave air pockets which subside later. Use something like an old fencing post about as thick as a wine bottle, or the best method is a drunken mark time by a big man with little feet.

Before depositing soil upon ground which has become firm by weathering, the surface should be stabbed up with

Design for a garden with a
cross-fall from west to east.

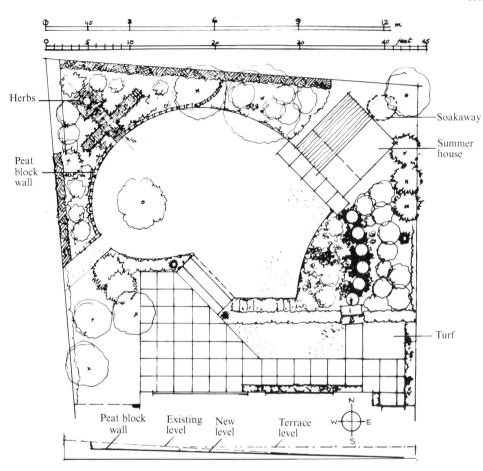

Herbs

Peat
block
wall

Soakaway

Summer
house

Turf

Peat block   Existing   New   Terrace
wall   level   level   level

a fork to avoid a hard 'pan' which
roots have difficulty in penetrating.

When time permits, made-up ground
should be allowed to weather and
settle so that any minor depressions
which appear during the period can be
corrected before the final surfacing
with turf, stone or gravel.

THE USE OF A SOAKAWAY

On this site (*above*), the house faces
north and there is a cross-fall from

west to east. The owner of the garden
had already bought a summerhouse
and the only place for this was the
north-east corner to capture most of
the sun. Because the drainage of water
down to the east meant that the east
side was water-logged, a deep hole
was dug and filled with rubble and
broken bricks in the north-east corner
to serve as a soakaway. The level on
the west side was reduced, but as it
was unwise to build up around the
trees on the east side, the subsoil was
carted away. Since the ground cut

Above, left: The site has been levelled and a low wall of peat blocks built.

Above, right: Planting has begun.

Below, left and right: The lawn has been sown and is already beginning to knit together.

away on the west side was lower than the natural level, the drop was accommodated by a wall of peat blocks; this left some slope to the east, but not as much as originally on the site. Later, the summerhouse was placed in front of the soakaway. As a precaution against water collecting along the east fence, the stepping-stones leading to the summerhouse were set in a sea of cobbles with spaces left for plants which like moisture, such as Astilbe,

Hemerocallis, Primulas, etc.

This garden also provides a useful illustration of the time factor. Here, the design was decided upon early in spring and the rest of the year spent in spare-time levelling and making a drainage soakaway. Planting was done in the following spring and the photographs taken in the summer. The lawn appeared in twelve days, and although immature in the photograph, it rapidly knitted up.

4 THE FRONT GARDEN

It is not uncommon to find houses set well back from the road with much more garden in front than behind. This arrangement and the aspect may make the front liable to be used for outdoor living, but in the majority of cases the chief function is to provide a setting for the building.

The keynote must be simplicity, though this does not mean that it should be dull or shapeless. Place a piece of glassware or china on a highly patterned and coloured cloth, and then on to a piece of plain or only lightly patterned material. Note how the second helps the ornament, while the first creates confusion by competing for attention. This same competition and confusion can arise in the settling of a house or bungalow into its site, and though one can find admirable examples of restraint, there are far too many gardens where the temptation to overdo the decoration has been too much. Walls serving no useful purpose or over-elaborate copings, pools, pergolas, concrete paths, ornaments, vases and figures create a conglomeration of inert material at the back of which is a small bungalow calling for acknowledgement.

The smaller the frontage the more the need for restraint, which is fortunate for both the pocket and the success of the scheme!

The house-purchaser often starts handicapped by finding a small patch of ground cut in two by the main entrance path and in some cases further reduced by a concrete run-in for the car. A concrete path next to the building, admittedly clean and tidy, leaves no room for an odd plant or climber, and the whole is made into a shallow box by an enclosing brick wall. Obviously, it is important to avoid adding further detail to destroy what little space remains.

Unfortunately, the most satisfying treatment of frontages is beyond the power of the individual to arrange, except in a limited way. Until such time as it becomes common practice to front all rows of houses with a tree-studded carpet of turf, maintained by the local authority, or by some other suitable arrangement, the householder must do the best he can with the small area under his control. It may be possible for two or more neighbours to combine and, by removing division fences, to develop such a treatment on their own, but failing this there are still ways in which the limited space of the individual plot can be preserved.

There is no real need to create a kind of defence position behind a brick boundary wall, except against neighbours' cats, dogs, and undisciplined children, which may be sufficient reason in some cases. When the house stands a little above pavement level, there is an opportunity to do some levelling to good effect. The area between building and pavement can

Front garden designed with a
minimal turning space near
the entrance.

Design for a plot where there is a great deal of space in front of the house.

be filled to make a broad terrace, the boundary wall serving only to retain the made-up ground, which is laid almost entirely with turf (or sown with seed) running right down to the top of the wall (*below*).

This open treatment is not only effective but is also an economy when the front wall has not already been built; but there will of course be many cases where conditions (front wall, paths, and so on) must be accepted as found. The same principle will apply:

avoid adding disturbing lines and shapes to cut up the space between boundary and house.

In the summer months a front ablaze with roses is always a pleasure, but such colour is best confined to borders leaving the maximum unbroken space for grass. The overall picture over the seasons must be considered, and turf, which has a warming effect even in winter, will be cooling in summer, especially if watered. Miniature patterns of dia-

A low terrace forms a restrained front garden.

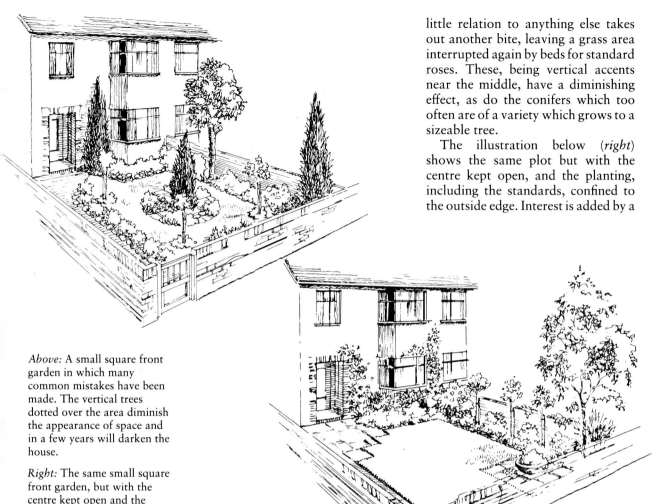

little relation to anything else takes out another bite, leaving a grass area interrupted again by beds for standard roses. These, being vertical accents near the middle, have a diminishing effect, as do the conifers which too often are of a variety which grows to a sizeable tree.

The illustration below (*right*) shows the same plot but with the centre kept open, and the planting, including the standards, confined to the outside edge. Interest is added by a

Above: A small square front garden in which many common mistakes have been made. The vertical trees dotted over the area diminish the appearance of space and in a few years will darken the house.

Right: The same small square front garden, but with the centre kept open and the planting confined to the outside edge.

mond or circular beds set in narrow strips of unmowable grass or thin ribbons of concrete are usually out of scale with the planting and the house, and can be confusing and difficult to maintain.

The illustration above (*left*) shows a 7·5m (25ft) square front garden containing some, but by no means all, of the common mistakes in treatment. The surrounding border on *four* sides of the open space first reduces it, then the large circular bed which bears

small feature comprising a low flower-filled bowl or trough, set on paving and cobble stones. The garden appears to belong to the house and sets it off. At the same time, being open, it preserves the width of the site.

There are occasions when it is impossible to maintain turf in nice condition, when for lack of time it cannot be given the attention it deserves, even when only a small patch is concerned. In such cases paving can be used, preferably laid with wide joints, and

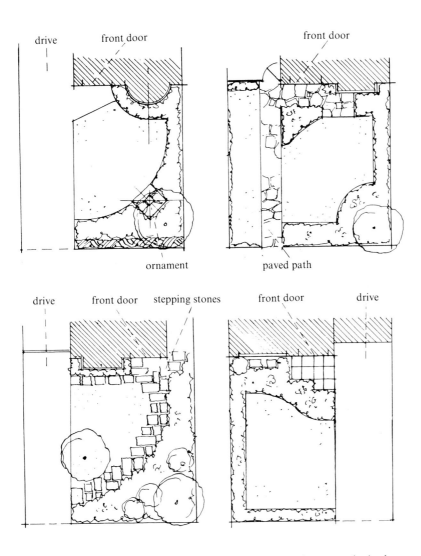

drive   front door

front door

ornament   paved path

drive   front door   stepping stones

front door   drive

Four outline plans for small front gardens. In each case an open centre is left.

with plenty of space left for rock plants. This will still require weeding, but perhaps not such urgent or tiring work as mowing.

Four outline plans of small front gardens are shown (*above*). In so small a piece of ground there is little room for fuss and detail, if there is to be unity between house and garden. Note the effort to preserve an open centre and the tendency for lines to flow across the plot rather than from road to building.

The wider front, with the house set farther back, offers more scope, but there is still a need for restraint if the extra space is not to be wasted.

ENTRANCE PATHS AND DRIVES

Quite a number of plots have two entrances – one for the car, another for foot traffic – sometimes along opposite side boundaries, but often run-

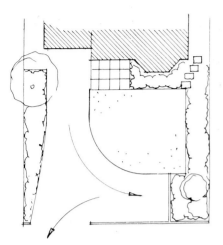

Above, left: A turning area sited immediately inside the entrance where reversing out is unsafe.

Above, right: A turning area placed to the front of the house.

ning parallel with very little ground in between. This has a narrowing effect, is a waste of good garden space, and, unless there is some very good reason for it, is best reduced to a single way-in to both garage and front door.

With a small car it is possible to manage with a 2·25m (7ft) width of drive if the run-in is short and straight; but a 2·75m (9ft) width is a more practical minimum, and even this is quite a slice from a small garden. When reversing out is unsafe, therefore, it is wise to reduce any turning space within the garden to the absolute workable minimum, and it is worth remembering that such an area need not be close to the house: it can be sited immediately inside the entrance (*above, left*). On a busy road it serves as a convenient pull-in for callers and tradesmen. The room needed will depend on a number of factors which are likely to vary for everyone: size of car, ability of driver, positioning of garage, width of doors, possible obstructions, and so on. By far the best way to decide is to forget the mathematics of turning circles and steering locks; take the car on to the site when the ground is hard enough, try out a few turns, and size the area

accordingly. On your plan it can be given a pleasing shape which satisfies the findings.

The one treatment guaranteed to fail in setting off the house is the arid-in-summer, bleak-in-winter sea of tarmacadam or gravel immediately in front of the building. When the car must be brought to the front door, or the drive must come in front of the house, an effort should be made to leave some garden between the two, preferably for a carpet of turf.

A forecourt big enough for a complete turn may look well with a sizeable building because the latter is big enough to be dominant, but in front of a small modern house it is quite out of proportion, distracting, and a great waste of space.

The fortunate few who have a say in the placing of the house do well to bear in mind that extra room on the garage side of the building can be put to good use in providing turning space which is clear of the main frontage. Others with rural sites might consider the possibility of crossing the front to turn beyond the house; but in crossing leave space between drive and building for turf and flower bed.

All surfaces that are to be subjected

to foot or vehicular traffic must be laid on a good foundation, the thickness of which will depend to some extent on the nature of the land, a firm well-drained sub-soil requiring least. A fair working minimum is 5cm (2in) for paving, 10cm (4in) for footpaths, and 15cm (6in) for drives; but when time and materials are available, these measurements might well be increased by half as much again. The purpose, of course, is to make a hard core which will prevent the formation of hollows in a pliable surface, or the tilting of paving stones, and at the same time to provide a drainage layer which will help to disperse water. Any hard clean material, broken brick, concrete or stone or clinker, can be employed, fine ash or coarse sand being worked into the interstices, and the whole rammed hard. As a temporary measure, and to spread the expense, this can be used as a surface while it weathers and settles.

Gravel and tarmacadam need an

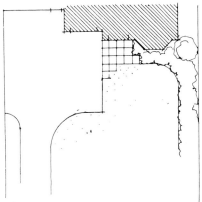

Extra room on the garage side can often be used to provide a turning space.

edging of some kind to prevent them spreading during consolidation and to retain the desired line or shape. This can be done with $2 \cdot 5 \times 15$cm (1×6in) creosoted boards fixed to pegs, with strips of stone or hard bricks laid on edge and set on cement, or with pre-cast 5×18cm (2×7in) concrete garden kerbing. Creosoted boards cost slightly less than concrete kerbs, but

A front garden with a low wall and a driveway along one side. The broken white line (across the lawn) shows extra space for a car, if needed.

are not so durable. Do not be persuaded to buy road-side kerbs, which, though efficient, are out of scale in a small garden.

The question of surface water must not be overlooked; paths can be given a camber, or (easier to lay) a side-to-side fall.

Gravel provides a pleasing, even and firm surface, but samples of the local material should be seen laid before ordering. It is referred to in some parts of the country as hoggin, and while the best contains sufficient natural binding to enable it to set to a hard finish, a poorer quality will disintegrate with wear.

Loose crushed stone chips make a path which is easy to lay, but it is not the easiest of materials on which to walk, and requires frequent raking to keep it looking tidy. Tarmacadam is well known, needs to be expertly laid, and though efficient is somewhat dull and depressing in appearance. It is best left for a year to settle, then sprayed with tar and dressed with pea shingle.

By following the maker's instructions carefully, the amateur has no difficulty in laying a surface which is an 'instant lay' macadam. It looks like 'tarmac' and spreads in a 8–10cm (3–4in) layer straight from the bag.

5 TERRACING AND STEPS

Not every house can have a terrace. One on a flat site loses little by this: it can still have open and possibly paved space round it, without the drop to lower ground implied by the word terrace. But on a sloping plot, nothing more becomes a house than an adequate terrace, on which it can rest with composure like a trophy on a plinth.

One has only to look at the simple diagrams below (*right*) to appreciate the sense of stability imparted by the provision of an area of level ground on each side of the building:

(a) A house standing on sloping ground. It appears ready to slide down-hill.

(b) Even a narrow wedge of levelled ground helps, though still too small to be really effective.

(c) A wider flat area has an immediate stabilizing effect.

(d) Planting on the terrace assists further.

There are no easy rules to follow when deciding the shape and size of a terrace; it is all a matter of judgement and of good proportions. So much depends, not only on the height of the house, but on its bulk and character, and the safest method is to draw out on plan what looks like a reasonable size, and roughly mark out on site with pegs and line. Then live with it for a few days and you will soon know whether it ought to be reduced or enlarged.

Size is important, but shape and treatment also need careful thought. Nothing looks worse than a terrace of a restless over-elaborated shape, worried by parapets and battlements, vases, urns, and pretentious piers.

Place a piece of tracing paper over the plan, trace the house and the side fences and, using a tee-square and set-square, if available, clearly mark the centre lines of the main windows. There may be a focal point on one of these which will give you a start.

The terrace forms a link between the house and the rest of the outdoor living space, and must therefore be shaped in harmony with the house plan. For example, a straight line across the site with steps down at any odd place, will not do. The only way in which this conforms is that the straight line might be parallel with the house, but it could equally well belong to any other building.

Four diagrams showing the need for terracing for a house on sloping ground: (b) limited terrace; (c) a larger terrace has a stabilising effect, especially with planting as in (d).

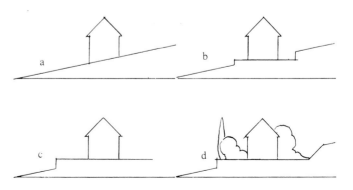

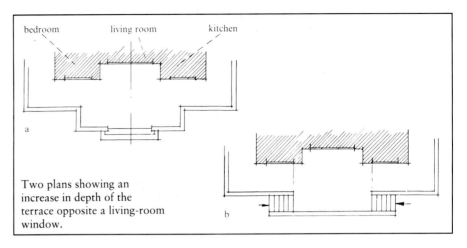

Two plans showing an increase in depth of the terrace opposite a living-room window.

Look for a moment at this part of a plan ((*a*), *above*) with bedroom and kitchen projecting, and living-room window set in a recess, with possibly a door or long window. This is likely to make the recess much used, especially if it faces the sun, and it would be natural to want more room here than elsewhere, so an increase in depth of terrace is desirable. A break forward in the terrace wall would be in keeping if it carried the line of the recess in the building, and if this should still not be enough then it might 'pick up' the ends or centres of the kitchen or bedroom windows. Alternatively, one might make the projecting portion the same width as the recess plus, on each side, an extra distance equal to the amount of the projection. In a case like this, where the building is symmetrical, or nearly so, the steps to the lower ground could be placed at the centre of the projection. With a drop of up to 60cm (2ft) they would be in proportion, but they should be made wide, remembering that long horizontal lines, in the direction of the width of the site, will assist in preserving that width.

For a greater drop, and especially when the lower ground is falling away, more steps are needed; the flight could become so weighty as to be out of proportion, more fitted to a mansion than a bungalow, so that it is better to descend sideways. Such an arrangement is shown (*above, b*): the steps fit into the projection of the terrace and are narrower. More of them reach out sideways to form a spreading feature balanced on the centre line.

The plan might very well be developed at some future date to form a feature incorporating a seat, or a small pool and fountain as in the sketch (*right*).

The bungalow, though symmetrical on plan, might not be so in elevation. There may be a gable end, or a hipped roof over the bedroom, and a flat over the projecting kitchen. Then one could be content with a single sideways flight, since symmetry is not forced on one by the façade of the building.

Suppose a bungalow with the same outline has a different arrangement of rooms. The portion in the recess might be the kitchen and the room on the left the main living room. The recess might for other reasons be unsuitable for sitting out. The terrace would then be shaped to give a greater area near the garden door from the living room. In this case a few steps could go almost on the corner, centred on the open space at the end of the house (*right*, (*a*)), or they could again be fitted into the angle of the projection as shown (*right* (*b*)).

The sideways descent is always worth considering, and can result not only in a satisfying design of steps but in a saving in the number required. If you are dropping to a lawn which slopes away and moving in the direction of the slope, each step takes you *down* but also *forward*; you are forever chasing the slope (*right*), adding step after step until the flight becomes a long narrow arm reaching out down the plot.

Variety in the outline of the terrace wall adds interest and enables you to give space where required for sitting, with economy in earth moving, when room is required merely to walk.

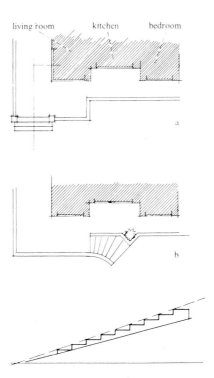

living room   kitchen   bedroom

Two plans for an asymmetrical terrace and steps where the main living-room is on the left.

Below, left: A terrace with steps on each side and a small pool and fountain at the base of the wall.

Below: Sideways descent of steps.

Left: A flight of steps chasing the slope.

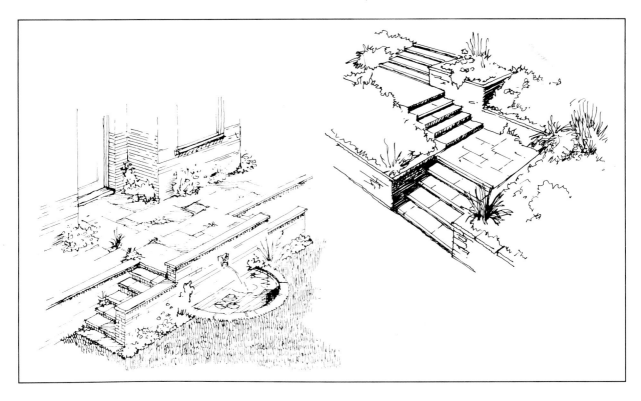

Design for terrace steps
turning into plot.

Opposite: In this garden
shallow steps lead obliquely
on to the lawn.

We have already given some thought
to the difficulty which arises when the
living-room window is close to the
boundary fence and, at the rough layout stage, have considered the advis-
ability of turning sharply into the plot
at the terrace steps (page 41). Now
that we are shaping the terrace, we
might see how this can be done. One
simple way is to place the steps opposite the window, but to tilt them to
establish the change in direction as
shown in (*a*) on page 83. In (*b*), (*c*),

and (*d*), a feature in the form of a low
bowl of planting, a small ornament or
an old stone sink is placed opposite
the window with the terrace wall suitably shaped, and the steps at an angle
to one side; (*e*) is a variation on (*a*)
with curved steps.

One should be careful about using
hard straight lines diagonally across
an open space, as would be the case
when a paved path cuts a lawn into
two awkward shapes; but when an
oblique line is part of the main shap-

ing and is a component part of the design rather than an incidental, there is good reason for using it. A small terrace built on the angle can be very effective especially if the slope on the ground is roughly at right-angles to it (*below (f)*). This could be developed even further by making the oblique line into a bold sweep or curve (*below (g)*).

Do not be afraid to make use of curves in the small garden. They can be restful and graceful, but they must be bold and clean, and any temptation to let them become mere wriggles should be resisted.

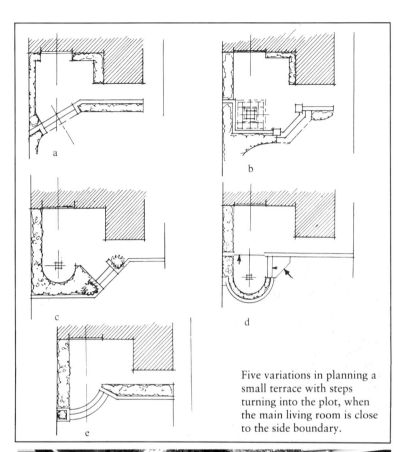

Five variations in planning a small terrace with steps turning into the plot, when the main living room is close to the side boundary.

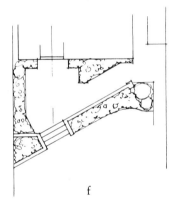

A small terrace built at an angle can be very effective: two variations in planning.

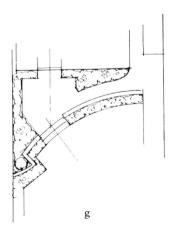

Site 1

On this site with a cross-fall, the land is higher on the right-hand side near the kitchen, falling across to the left-hand fence. The ground in front of the living-room window can be made up, while it is left very much as existing on the right or perhaps only reduced slightly. The lawn is cut into this raised ground, the excavated material being used to make up on the left near the building. This higher ground on the right really becomes part of the terrace and, if there is also some fall in the length of the plot, the space next to the right-hand fence can be reshaped to give a long slow ramp for a service path. At the centre of the curved end of the terrace, but at lawn level, a small pool or ornament might be added later.

Site 2

With the fall from left to right, the higher ground on the left is this time carried through under the kitchen window and terminated in a semi-circular end, hedged in to screen a small utility or herb patch between the end of the terrace and the right-hand fence.

Site 3

With certain contemporary houses of asymmetrical design free curves, those which flow with an ever-changing centre of curvature and radius, can be used. They are best drawn freehand, the aim being to design a clean, graceful shape which belongs to the building, and set off its often severe lines. The most striking effects can be obtained from the juxtaposition of curved and straight lines.

TURF ON THE TERRACE

Good quality turf can provide a dignified and faultless accompaniment to good architecture. It has its limitations of course: it will show signs of wear if subjected to heavy use; wet after dew can make it slippery; it needs feeding, mowing throughout the growing season and watering in dry weather; but it is inexpensive and can therefore be used in quantity. The point to remember with turf is that you are dealing with living plants which have the same needs as other plants: good soil, light, air and water. So designing for the material, you will as always ensure that these conditions are satisfied.

Nothing sets off a house so well as a carpet of green grass, but it is important to design the areas big enough to be mown by machine. Strips less than about 45cm (18in) wide are a

Site 1: design for a terrace on ground where there is a cross-fall from right to left.

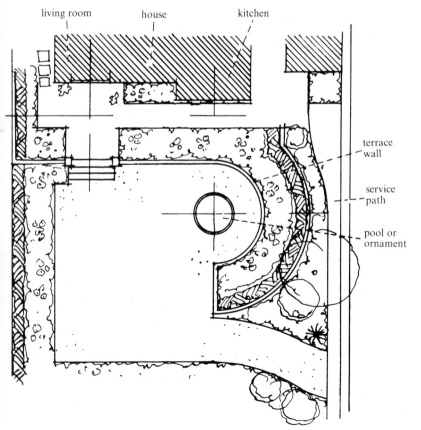

living room   house   kitchen

terrace wall

service path

pool or ornament

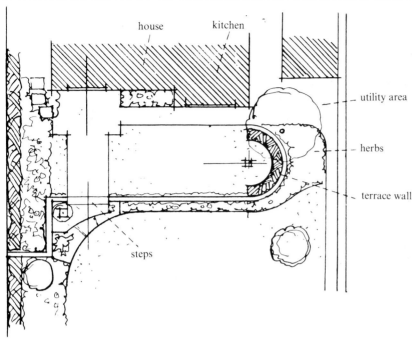

house   kitchen

utility area

herbs

terrace wall

steps

Left: Site 2: design for a
terrace where the cross-fall is
from left to right.

Below: Site 3: design for a
terrace with free curves to set
off a house of contemporary
design.

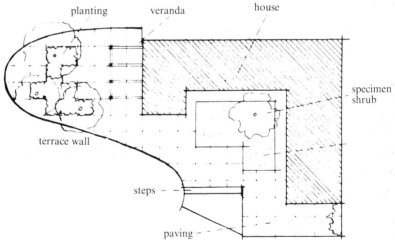

planting   veranda   house

specimen
shrub

terrace wall

steps

paving

nuisance, for they become distorted
by edging and one finally resorts to
shears. Grass cannot be carried right
up to the face of the building where it
is difficult to operate the mower or
used directly at the foot of steps or on
narrow paths where continual traffic
on the same spot causes undue wear.
A good practical point is to make turf
level at least 25mm (1in) above that of
adjacent paving or gravel so that the
mower can overlap without damage
to the cutters. Deep edges are easier to
trim with long-handled shears as there
is depth for the lower blade to slide
under the whiskers of grass. Grass
areas and verges on the terrace may be
sown, the edges being retained by a
batten of timber later removed when
the grass roots have knitted, or use can
be made of the metal strips now sold
for the purpose. A less tidy way is to
allow the soil on which the grass is
sown to spread over the adjacent surface by 25–50mm (1–2in) and, when
the sward has developed, to cut off the
surplus (*right*).

One clear essential, though one so
often overlooked, is that if turf is to be
kept smart it must be even. Undulation is in order on a lawn, but knobs
and potholes pitch the mower about
and result in an uneven crop.

Below: An overlapping grass
edge is easily trimmed with a
'half moon' edging iron.

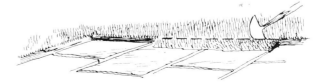

Good quality turf, sharply
edged.

Pavement plants: tufts of
pinks and thyme.

PAVING ON THE TERRACE

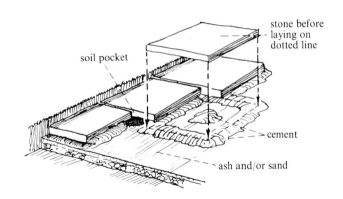

Stone is the cleanest of paving materials, and used close to the house as the last surface on which one treads before entering, it helps to prevent grit being carried in on the shoes. The charm of stone, however, lies in its being a home for rock plants: even a small patch, laid with wide joints and occasional pockets where rise tufts of thrift and pinks with splashes of prostrate thyme reaching across the surface, can be a source of great pleasure. It always seems a lost opportunity, then, to lay stone with the joints filled with cement ironed to a smooth face, the whole taking on the appearance of an internal floor; one might just as well use cement throughout. No one designing a garden will want to make unnecessary work, but there are some gardening tasks that are essential if the enchantment admired in the work of others is to be created. The care of paving is one of these; weeds will grow in the crevices and must be removed, but there are ways of reducing the work to a minimum.

The ground on which paving is laid must be clean. If left, couch roots, bellvine or ground elder will throw up shoots between the stones. Another aid is to lay the stone on a firm layer of 8cm (3in) or so of ash, cinders, broken stone or sand, which also forms a drainage stratum, and to bed each stone on cement with a continuous pad of it where joints occur. Here and there, at the junction of two or more stones, a pocket is made in the ash layer, filled with good soil and the cement kept clear. The joints, however, are not pointed up with cement, but have sand or soil brushed in, and any weed which seeds there is easily removed.

Because of its colour, durability and clean natural face, York stone has always been the most popular paving medium in spite of its high cost in some areas. To obtain the best effect from rectangular slabs of varying sizes, two seemingly small points should be borne in mind: do not allow more than three stones to line up on one joint; break the continuity with a slab across. Ensure that all joints are parallel; the effect of stones pointing in slightly different directions can be restless.

Above: Laying paving on an ash or sand bed with cement.

Below: In laying paving, ensure that all joints are parallel as in A and C. Joints out of parallel, as in B, can be restless.

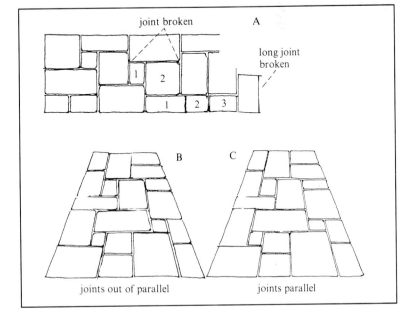

Laying crazy paving.

When, in the interests of economy, the cheaper form of the same material – crazy paving – must be used, it is best arranged with the larger pieces down the centre of a path or, where there is most traffic on an open area, with medium-sized stones as an edging, and the remainder filled in with the smallest (*above*).

Since paving can become 'greasy' when wet or under trees, it should not be laid on a slope where it would be dangerous.

There are, of course, in various parts of the country, other stones which merit attention and enquiries should always be made regarding the local material, which can be responsible for a great saving in cost over York.

There are good artificial stones available in rectangular slabs, some made from crushed York stone, others which have a grey concrete core with a layer of tinted cement 'icing', and some coloured all through. These are often manufactured in multiples of a basic size, a fact to be remembered when designing paths with artificial stone in mind. These varying sizes can be laid in a pattern rather like natural stone, but are of course more regular and somewhat mechanical in general appearance.

Granolithic slabs, such as are used on street pavements, represent the most economical form of precast paving. They do not pretend to be anything but concrete and are very slow to weather.

Concrete paving can be cast on the site and screeded between battens. It should be left plain and not scratched to represent crazy paving; this is a common practice, but to be deplored since it is quite meaningless and ineffectual. Nor is it advisable to brush the surface to expose the shingle aggregate or press stones into the surface; it may look interesting, but is dangerous to walk on, particularly with nailed shoes.

Rather than score marks to look like slabs, it is better to lay down battens on edge in a framework over a small section, fill in the concrete screeded level and, before it finally hardens, carefully prise out the battens (to be used again) leaving open joints later to be filled with soil or weak cement (*below*).

Battens in place for casting concrete slabs. The open joints can later be filled with soil.

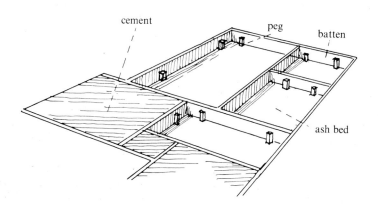

cement

peg

batten

ash bed

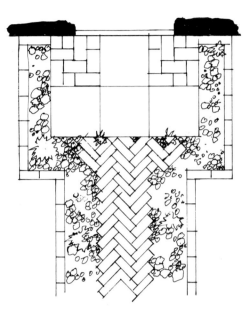

Left: Using old roofing tiles for paving.

Far left: Using bricks laid flat in a square and on edge to make herring-bone patterns.

Other materials especially suited to the small garden and to small areas are bricks, tiles, granite setts and cobble stones. Hard burnt, or engineering bricks, which will not disintegrate in frost, should be used, laid flat with the 225 × 115mm (9 × 4½in) face showing or on edge in a square or herringbone pattern. Old plain roofing tiles laid on edge with cement make an interesting surface but, since only the edge of the tile shows and the laying is tedious, they are best used over small areas only as part of a pattern. In some parts of the country, however, it is possible to obtain old flooring tiles or quarries, often 22·5 or 30·5cm (9 or 12in) square. These are not always weatherproof and ones with cracks or apparent weakness should be discarded.

There is no weathering trouble with stone setts or cobble stones. The former being roughly cubical and heavy can be laid 'dry', but are better on cement in places where they will be subjected to wheeled traffic. Cobbles, too, can be tapped into the soil, but to eliminate weeding a carpet of cement forms a good bed. It is important not to let the cement show and, once set,

to top off with sand or soil. Both these materials give interesting relief to large areas of gravel or tarmacadam as, for instance, when they are used to form a gutter on each side of the drive.

With all these hard paving materials, the surface must be checked continually during laying, since a brick or the corner of a stone standing up slightly can be a dangerous trip. Although plenty of cement will not impair the efficiency of paving, it certainly spoils the appearance and is best kept out of sight; it should be used with only as much water as it required to make it workable, and with the greatest care taken to prevent smearing of the face of the paving material, stone or cobbles, or whatever may be in use.

The Cost of Paving

The cost of natural stone paving must obviously vary according to the distance from the source of supply. York stone, for example, may be reasonable in the north of England, but expensive when haulage is added. Rectangular slabs in random sizes are sold by the area, crazy paving or broken slabs of irregular shape are sold by weight.

Old worn slabs from city streets can be bought for less than the freshly quarried material. They are serviceable but, being sometimes very thick and hollowed by wear, it is best to see them before buying. They can be heavy to handle.

In the south of England, an alternative is Portland stone, a by-product from the sawing up of masonry blocks. It is cheaper, and varies a lot in thickness. It can be used for crazy paving or cut for walling, but becomes slippery under trees. It is 'white' in colour, but soon weathers.

Several excellent artificial stone garden slabs, best seen before deciding, are available at half the cost of York, and even less are the Granolithic pavement slabs.

PLANTING ON THE TERRACE

It is desirable to have planting on the terrace but important to restrict it to the edges so that the middle is left open for circulation. Beds should conform to the lines of the house: not necessarily following every break or set back in the wall as a ribbon-like strip, but with reasonable formality (*left*).

If you are afraid of flower-beds making the house damp, a strip of paving can be laid between bed and wall, though with modern construction there is little danger of damp, you keep ground level two brick courses below damp-proof course. Remember the window cleaner and lay odd stepping stones in the bed for his use whenever a wide bed is made under a window.

A RAMP FOR SERVICING

Though it is usual and indeed interesting to descend from the terrace to the lawn by nicely proportioned steps, at the kitchen or service end of the house a ramp is sensible, if only for easy barrowing. Where this side of the house is on the high side of the site there is little difficulty as the terrace wall peters out into natural ground level (*left*); but with a slope the other way it will be necessary to give some thought to an easy way down, possibly by stopping the terrace short (*far left*); or by such arrangements as are shown here in diagrammatic form on page 91.

Below: A plan for small beds on a terrace.

Bottom, left: In this diagram the terrace has been ended short so as to allow a ramp for a barrow.

Bottom, right: A ramp for a barrow from the terrace to the lawn at one corner is often useful at the service end of the house.

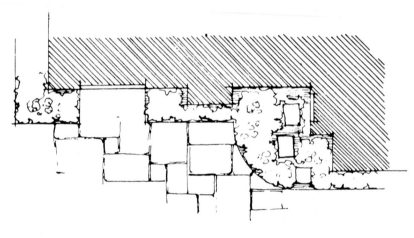

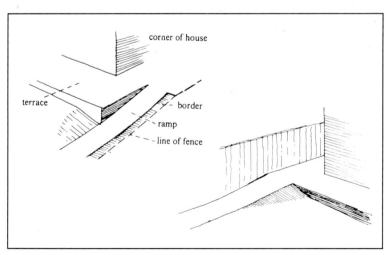

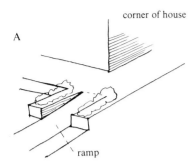
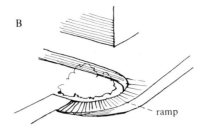
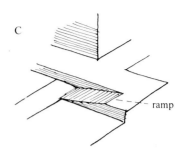

corner of house

A   ramp

B   ramp

C   ramp

LAND RISING FROM THE HOUSE

So far we have been thinking in terms of land falling away from the house at the back, but such conditions do not always apply; the land may fall towards the house, and we must consider treatment for these cases.

I have known gardens where the slope has been left, but sooner or later the oppression of the ground descending on the building has been too much and measures have been taken to create some space. A good deal of earth-moving is involved and the effectiveness of the treatment will depend to some extent on just how much one is

Three diagrams showing possible arrangements for a ramp from terrace to lawn.

In this garden the land rises away from the house.

willing and able to do. If the ground rises at the back it is likely to be falling at the front, and much of the excavated material can be wheeled round to make up there. The rate of incline will naturally affect what is done, but the principle object is to clear some levelled space round the house big enough to move about on without climbing. It is better to rise in easy stages with low banks or walls, one behind the other, leaving room for walking and planting on the intermediate terraces than to level out a big area and then step up to original ground with an enormous bank or wall.

Carving into Rising Land

The carving away of soil can make new and interesting shapes as in the two designs sketched below. These two formal treatments take the rise in a series of low walls and/or banks, but with the sun on the slope the site can lend itself to an informal treatment, even a modest rock outcrop. In these cases it is still wise to have some ground near the house at a level 2 brick courses below the damp proof course before starting to rise, and then the slope, if it is even, must be modelled to give it variation and interest. Provision must also be made to start

Right: Land rising away from the house taken in easy stages.

Below: A small terrace with a seat, when the land rises away from the house.

with for planting to screen out as many as possible of the hard surrounding lines, such as fences and neighbours' houses. This can really only be done when in full sun; otherwise, planting screening out the neighbours will also put the rock garden into shadow.

Few sites have only one problem to be overcome: for example, a house may stand on rising land; it may also be the last house in the row and alongside a minor road; the plot may even taper.

To avoid the expenses of a 2m (6ft) high wall or boarded fence to secure privacy, a belt of trees could be planted 3m (10ft) apart with a view to thinning out at a later date. These could be reinforced with shrubs such as the common laurel, *Berberis stenophylla*, *Cotoneaster lacteus*, and *Elaeagnus ebbingei* planted 1·5m (5ft) apart, again with a view to a little thinning as required at a later date. Trees and shrubs not only filter out dust but also provide a sound baffle. The trees will take time to grow to a reasonable height, but some privacy could be secured immediately with a wing of trellis or framed-up sheets of translucent plastic. The rising ground could be dealt with by making a sunk terrace at a level two courses below the damp-proof course, with a slight fall from the house and gulleys to take away surface water. This would cut into the rising ground, which could be retained by low walls of brick or stone. It might also be necessary to put in two or three steps (as indicated at A and more at B in the drawing below), the land being graded into the natural slope.

Further design points to notice in

Sketch of design for garden in which the land rises from the house; see page 94 for plan.

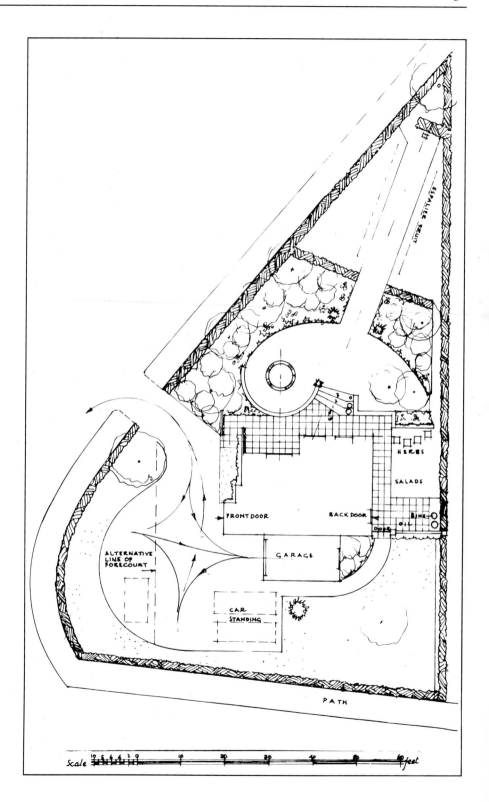

Plan for garden where land
rises away from house.

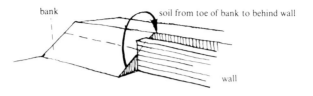

this plan (*left*) are that the steps radiate from the centre point of the pool which is opposite the centre of the loggia; a turf path runs up to the end of the plot flanked by espalier fruit trees trained on wire and terminates with a white seat against a yew hedge.

BAD PRACTICE TO BE AVOIDED

Quite often when taking over a new house expenses are so crippling that purchases of materials for garden construction have to be curtailed, and temporary expedients have to be used. Do try to avoid half measures or compromises that you will later regret. Instead of walls, do *not* use odd lumps of broken concrete, or other hard material to hold up your change in level, by making what is usually called a rockery as opposed to a rock bank or rock outcrop (see page 168). The rockery is an anachronism, a relic from a period when people delighted in grottoes of sea shells, quartz and coloured bottles stuck together to make something 'pretty'. It has neither dignified formality, nor the freedom of the naturalistic, but somehow has become accepted as a feature which no garden should be without. No one will deny the beauty of Alpine plants, but they, pathetic things, can only assert themselves when they have effectively smothered the medium in which they are forced to grow. Quite apart from the fact that it is a perfect home for weeds, what beauty or reason can there be in a conglomeration of broken concrete, stone or slag, often mixed, and plastered on a heap of soil or a bank like almonds on a cake?

Instead, make a neat bank of grass with a definite clean edge at top and bottom. It means difficult mowing,

but it is worth it and, if a flat of grass is made 90–120cm (3–4ft) wide on the top level, a small hand-mower can be pushed down the slope. At a later date it is a fairly simple job to cut away the bottom half of the bank, build a wall and pack the excavated material behind it; but you may in time grow to like your grass bank so much that the wall will never be built.

A bank, provided it is not too steep – the shallower the better – and is made with good soil, can be clothed with prostrate growing shrubs and, in lime-free areas, heathers. As a temporary measure a drop can be accommodated by a turf wall – old turves from the site cut 30cm (1ft) wide, and laid one on top of the other like bricks, presenting a fairly even face from which grass will grow.

DEEP KERBS

When the drop is no more than about 45cm (18in), it is possible to use Granolithic slabs, such as those laid on street pavements. These are good value, especially if second hand. They are set almost vertical with a cant towards the higher ground, and buried as much as the drop will allow. When there is a danger of pressure on the higher ground due to its continual use as a path, the tendency for the slaps to overturn can be corrected by setting the bottom edge in concrete with a 'toe' which is covered with soil. The top edges of the slabs are of course set to a clean straight line (*right*).

Replacing a grass bank with a wall: the soil from the lower part of the bank is packed behind the wall.

Use of large slabs on edge for holding up a grass terrace, where the drop is not more than 45cm (18in). For extra support the base of the slab can be set in concrete as in the section.

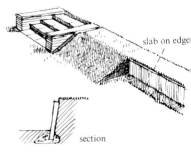

STEPS

When the house stands high relative to the road or a private drive-in, and when one approaches the door through a right-angled turn, it is best to level up the ground outside the door. The higher ground can then be retained by a neat wall in brick or artificial stone-walling blocks. There are a number of ways of dealing with the lead-in. One would be to lay strips of 'stone', each slightly higher than the other, with the spaces between slabs filled with cobbles (*right*). This is really a slope, but without the danger of having to walk on slippery stones on the tilt in winter months or wet weather. Three radial steps take one up to the top level. Another solution would be to make the path in tar macadam or shingle edged with cobble stones and treat the steps either in concrete, stone, or brick on edge, all of which are shown here (*below*). If the difference in level is no more than 65cm (2ft), the retaining wall can be done in precast concrete 60 × 90cm (2 × 3ft) slabs set almost vertically with the lower edge bedded in buried concrete. The face of the vertical slabs can be unified by a slurry of cement, and if necessary coloured to match the house.

Steps in the small garden can be a feature and present an opportunity for some craftsmanship, though they must first be properly designed, otherwise a great deal of effort and expense will be wasted. The two important points are width and size. It is irritating to have to use steps in single file, apart from the fact that narrow steps as a main route look puny. Over-steep steps with inadequate foothold are not only tiring but can be dangerous, since one must look down and exercise care in negotiating them.

Retaining wall made from pre-cast concrete slabs set almost vertically with the lower edge buried in bedded concrete (as shown also on page 95).

Left: Pathway made on a slope made from strips of 'stone', each laid slightly higher than the other, with the space between the slabs filled with cobbles.

Below: (clockwise from top left): steps forward of a retaining wall; steps made from logs drilled and spiked to the ground; old railway sleepers used as risers; steps turning through 90 degrees; steps can be made from discs of concrete or slices of tree trunks.

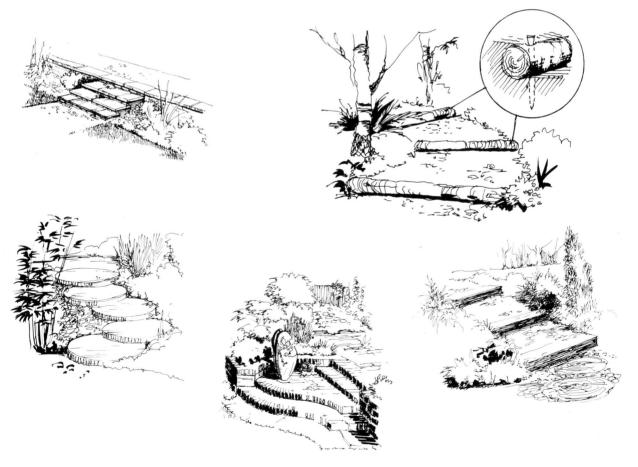

Thyme bank with tree-stump steps.

Garden steps should literally be taken in one's stride. 12cm (5in) is ample rise for each, and anything over a 15cm (6in) rise becomes a real effort. When space permits, it is better to add an extra step reducing the rise of each to 11cm (4½in) or even 10cm (4in). Obviously everyone does not take the same stride and a little latitude is permissible, but for easy ascent make the tread (or the horizontal part on which the foot is placed) about 35cm (14in) for a 12cm (5in) rise increasing it to 38cm (15in) for a 11cm (4½in) rise and 40cm (16in) for a 10cm (4in) rise.

It is important, even if one has not reached the stage of working out structural detail, to appreciate how much room a flight of steps can take. The kind of questions you will find yourself asking are: Can the steps bite into the body of the terrace or can a few or all of them project beyond the main terrace wall? Are the steps which project beyond the wall so far above the lower ground that they need the protection of a flanking wall and, if so, should this have a level top or be raked down with the run of the steps? The answers are yours; it all depends on

Suggested dimensions for easy steps.

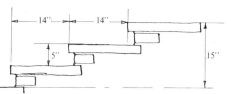

Stone steps: the width willingly sacrificed to the invasion of dianthus.

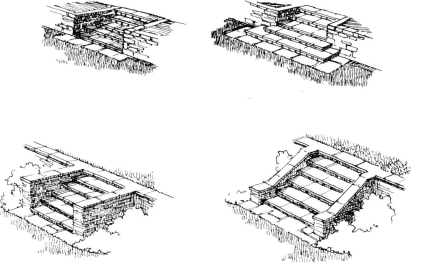

Steps can often be arranged to bite into a terrace (*far left*). Alternatively, a few steps may project beyond the terrace wall.

Two more designs for steps projecting beyond a wall.

your own conditions, your own preferences, the materials available and whether you will build them yourself or enlist a little part-time skilled assistance.

If you want to see the terrace wall from the inside, it can be carried up to sitting height about 38cm (15in), though naturally this uses up more material. It is safer when the drop is steep, but a certain amount of protection can be ensured by stopping the terrace wall at terrace level and planting a low hedge behind it. When de-

signing for a house with long, low lines and not too much drop to the lawn, a restful effect is obtained by having a flat coping to the wall and by bringing turf on the terrace right up to it but 4cm (1½in) higher to facilitate mowing and to provide a clean edge.

Avoid too many piers in your wall and steps design. They add strength, but with low walls it is quite unnecessary to build a pier at every angle and terminal of the wall. The whole effect becomes too heavy and fussy, and it complicates building.

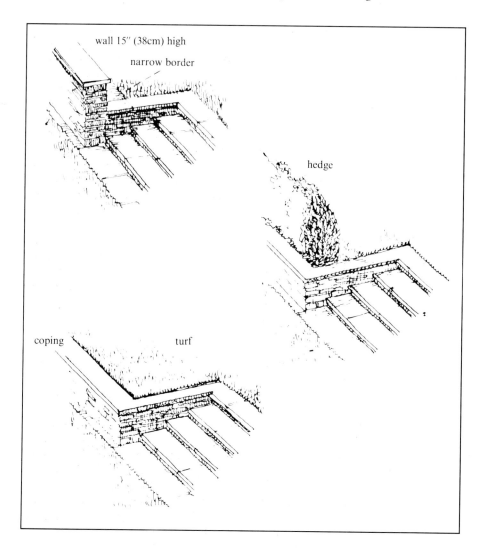

Designs for a terrace wall and steps.

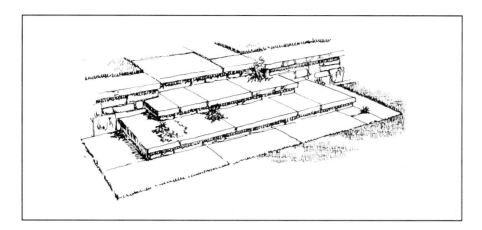

Design for a terrace wall and steps.

MATERIALS FOR WALLING

Garden walling offers scope for ingenuity in the use of materials and often something unusual bought at a favourable price can be made to serve. The customary materials vary in price according to the distance from source. Stone is expensive and best used for walls only in or near districts where there is indigenous rock. There, good examples can be seen, and local merchants will be able to quote for the material on the basis of your calculation of the face area of your proposed walls.

Stone varies from irregular 'lumps' to stratified stone which can be laid in courses with mortar, or 'dry' (without mortar). The cost increases as labour is put into each piece, i.e. the trimming of the ends and 'dressing' of the face. Stone with strata should always be laid on its natural bed and not on edge.

Re-constituted York stone and similar artificial blocks cost less and are easy to handle, while even cheaper are old snapped pavement slabs (laid flat) – dull but efficient.

Bricks vary from the cheapest, the well-known 'Fletton', to good quality facing bricks at four times the price, and in between are second-hand bricks from external work.

Flettons used for retaining walls should be backed by waterproofed cement or bitumen to prevent absorption of moisture and disintegration, and there are proprietary sprays to waterproof the face. Near the house use a brick the same or similar to the building.

Boundary and division wall panels can be built to a height of 2m (6ft) in concrete blocks. They need to be strengthened at 2·5m (8ft) intervals by piers. The whole can be colour-washed or finished with a slurry of slightly fluid cement. Notched Fletton bricks can be used in the same way. They take a rendering well, but that is skilled work better done by a craftsman.

Concrete has many uses in the modern garden, and the Cement and Concrete Association publish fully informative booklets on the subject, available at builders' merchants, garden centres and specialist retail outlets. For the beginner, *Concrete round your house and garden* is particularly useful. You can obtain a free copy by writing *on a postcard* to Publications Distribution, Cement and Concrete Association, Wexham Springs, Slough SL3 6PL and quoting the reference number 93.101.

Right: When planting shrubs
and trees, adequate space
must be allowed for them to
develop to maturity. Note the
easy, shallow steps.

Opposite: A border of
intriguing irregularity, with
both tall and small plants
spilling over on to the paths.

6 PLANT FORM

It is a common misapprehension to think that a garden is first 'made' and the planting added afterwards as decoration. On the contrary: the design of beds and borders involves constant reflection on the plants to be used. In the early stages we are not so concerned about the actual trees or shrubs, but the type of plant, its size and shape, and the outline it will present when developed.

Except with the smallest plots, which are seen chiefly from the house, one must usually design for more than one viewpoint, and just as the work of the sculptor is satisfying from all angles so plant grouping must offer pleasing and everchanging compositions as one walks through the garden. Beds must therefore not merely look right as ground pattern, but provide areas specially positioned and shaped for the type of plant to be grown.

The shrubbery will be neither a bed where shrubs are planted at random nor one where they are in orderly rows, rising evenly from small at the front to large at the back. The smaller plants will be in drifts or groups, each of which will be slightly apart from the next but close enough for the plants to be good neighbours, making a wave of foliage from which rises a larger plant. Here and there the bigger ones will come forward towards the front of the border, creating protective bays for something needing shelter, a splash of herbaceous colour,

Right: A small bed in outline arranged for planting with summer bedding.

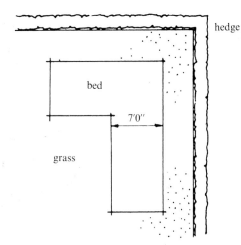

or a patch of lilies. At intervals in the middle depth, and at the back, a small tree will lift the whole well above eye-level.

Hedges, sometimes consigned to plan as a scribbled line of uncertain thickness, must be given enough room to develop according to the nature of the plant to be used: never less than 60cm (2ft) and as much as 3m (10ft) for a plant like laurel. This is so often mutilated to a shorn miserable wall, when it might be a handsome bank of foliage if allowed to grow to a size in proportion to its leaf.

Though you may no longer be interested when a tree has grown to maturity, it should be planted so that even if it becomes a problem, calling for some redesigning of a garden, it will never be a nuisance or a danger to the house.

A little discreet and purposeful observation in any residential district will provide examples, not only of good planting, but also of its misuse, particularly in relation to the siting of trees. A cedar or a weeping willow,

charming and decorative in the young state, graces the tiny patch in front of many a house. Cherries, crabs and laburnums so close that their heads are touching, shrubs which have outgrown their positions, all show lack of thought in the early stages of the garden planning.

A shrub group can be unsatisfactory unless it is designed as such. For example, suppose the bed (*above*) is part of a plan. It is eventually filled with summer bedding of negligible height, and the general effect is as in the sketch (*left*). So far so good. Later, however, it may be filled with a few odd shrubs to save seasonal restocking, and though as individual plants the shrubs are attractive, the overall effect is somewhat uninteresting (*below*). Had the bed been designed

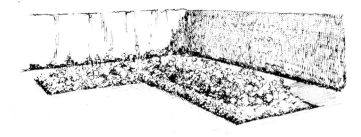

Above: The same bed planted with low-growing summer annuals.

Right: A few shrubs have now been planted in the bed to save seasonal restocking, but the overall effect is still rather uninteresting.

The same bed designed with a curved edge and arranged from the beginning for the heights to lead up to a small tree near the centre. It would appear more interesting at all seasons.

originally with shrubs in mind, with thought to the modelling of the group, it might have looked as above. But in order to accommodate such grouping, the bed would have been made of greater depth in places and given a softer outline more in keeping with the plants contained (*below*).

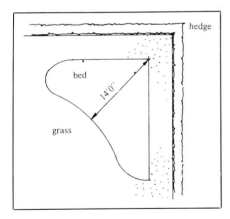

PLANT USES

Plants can have various roles in the making of a garden:

Hedges

Plants in close, regular repetition form a hedge which can be clipped to simu-

late a wall, or be allowed to grow freely. It will be used to define boundaries and for the internal division of space. There is a wide variety, but experience has shown that some plants are more adaptable than others, and selection will depend on position, price, speed of growth, suitability to soil and climate, and, of course, on one's own preference (see above page 56).

Screening

Trees grouped closely form a copse or spinney of inestimable value in the masking of unsightly buildings or the provision of privacy. With the addition of underplanting, screening can be secured at all levels. Generally speaking, the nearer a screening plant is to the viewer the better; a shrub a few yards distant will often be as effective as a tree farther away, so close temporary plants can be made to serve while distant trees grow.

Far left: The outline of the bed redesigned with a curved edge.

Below: A shrub or small tree a few yards distant will screen a distant building as effectively as much larger trees farther away.

Shrubs and trees can be used to break up space and add perspective, without reducing the garden into separate compartments.

Much of what one does to avoid seeing out will also serve to prevent outsiders seeing in, but the owner of the small town garden overlooked by tall buildings has a special problem often solved by selecting trees for their wide spread rather than their height.

In cases where space is limited, one aid is the training of trees to grow towards each other, the outward-growing branches being removed. This 'pleaching' is done with such trees as limes to produce a formal band of foliage at a high level.

Screen trees will also provide a windbreak, and as an incidental benefit will filter out a certain amount of dust and have a muffling effect on sound. Planted as a screen, trees can be grouped more closely than would be the case if they were to be allowed to develop as specimens, especially if they are the same kind of tree. At 3m (10ft) apart, they would tend to draw each other up to slender proportions and at some later date thinning of

about half might be needed, but the shelter provided in the early stages of the garden's life makes this worth while.

Coniferous trees may well be included or used alone, but when mixed with hardwoods, it is best to keep them in a band of their own, breaking into the deciduous trees in a ragged line and avoiding hard regular rows throughout whenever possible.

When trees are close, avoid a jumble of kinds: a group of cherry stems making one head is beautiful; a cherry, a crab and a laburnum struggling for space make a restless and pathetic sight.

Space division

Even in the small plot the main body of the garden need not be wide open, to be scanned at a glance, and the careful use of shrubs and trees will break up space without reducing it to separate compartments. A spur of planting curling out into the lawn from a side border will do this, and a small group of birches with several stems and one head allows a glimpse between the trunks to engender the intriguing feeling that there is something beyond worth seeing.

Framing the View

The view, when one exists, can be borrowed, so to speak, by framing with suitable trees and by the use of planting to take the eye to the 'picture'.

Complementing the House

The house dominating the site must be anchored, and its fusion with the garden effected by planting at its base, sometimes on its walls, and by the soft irregularity of tree and shrub foliage

acting as a foil to the severity of its
lines.

The restrained use of trees with an
architectural character in the garden
will have a unifying influence.

Shade and Background

There is no shade so pleasant as that
provided by a tree, probably because
of the constant movement of air
through the branches; nor is there any
sight quite so peaceful as the long
shadows of trees across a lawn in the
evening sun. Apart from this, there is
great pleasure to be experienced from
the play of light through foliage,
creating dark silhouettes against a
high-light, or a sparkle of sunlit
leaves displayed against the contained
shadow of the deeper foliage.

The aesthetics of shape and texture
are doubly enjoyable when foliage
colour is also present, or when bright
splashes are added to the composition by foreground flowers glowing
against the deep tone of evergreens.

1 Rounded

2 Upright or fastigiate

3 Weeping

4 Horizontal

5 Decorative

Plant forms

Plant Drapery

Whenever it is necessary to use trellis, wherever there is an arch, a pier, or an expanse of brickwork, one turns to climbing plants, of which there is such a wealth. The most stubborn of hard lines can be broken by their softening influence, and some quite ugly and immovable construction merely draped, and not hidden, ceases to be an eyesore.

There are many other plant uses: the punctuation of an unbroken lawn; the clothing of banks and slopes, shaped to become a feature instead of merely a means of accommodating a change in level; the camouflage of such necessary blemishes as the septic tank, are small but no less important functions.

CLASSIFICATION BY SHAPE AND SIZE

Everyone has his own liking for special plants, for reasons sometimes difficult to explain and sometimes unimportant. Yours (given the right conditions) will no doubt appear in your garden. Leaving these aside, your first requirement as someone designing a garden and looking for structural material is to find plants of the right shape and size.

Look over a well-established garden, such as your own local park, or even a natural landscape, and see the variety of tree shapes. They are not simply trees, but trees with their own characteristic outline and habit. You may not know all their names but you will be able to match them, some so alike in every detail that they must be the same, others alike in general rough outline but with differences of foliage or colour which point to their being different trees.

A classification of all possible shapes would be a complicated affair, but it is possible to group plants under five headings by allowing a good deal of latitude within each conventional outline. These are:

1 Rounded

The common, softly rounded outline of such trees as beech, oak, lime, elm; by no means all the same, as it includes oval, egg, or pear shapes, but similar enough to be summed up in a child's representation of a tree.

2 Upright or fastigiate

The noticeable, fastigiate or upright grower with upstretched branches. Included in this generally vertical shape are conical and fastigiate conifers, Lombardy poplar, cypress and the upright beech often known as Dawyck Beech.

3 Weeping

The weeping tree with naturally pendant branches as exemplified by the weeping willow. This group includes certain trees of upright growth but with branchlets which drip and plants which make a dome shape.

4 Horizontal

Trees which grow outwards with a strong horizontal line in their structure similar to the lamination of the cedar of Lebanon.

5 Decorative

This group is best described as 'decorative' and includes plants possibly already under other headings, but which have some special characteristic such as unusual growth, bark, foliage, e.g. Maidenhair tree (*Gink-*

go *biloba*), *Prunus serrula tibetica, Eucalyptus.*

Size

Within each shape group there will be a range of sizes, and as our application is to the garden we must think of trees and shrubs together, and of their ultimate development.

Environment has such an influence on the welfare of a plant that it is unwise to assume that a certain tree will reach a given height in a given time. One can find identical trees growing in the same garden under what are apparently the same conditions, one outstripping the other. Furthermore some people have difficulty in visualizing tree sizes in terms of metres or feet, preferring some comparative scale such as the height of the

Table showing trees and shrubs of different forms and sizes.

	Forest trees LARGE	Garden trees MEDIUM	Large shrubs SMALL	Small shrubs DWARF
	Ash Beech Oak Lime Horse chestnut Sweet chestnut Norway maple Birch	Thorn Crab Cherry (Japanese) Laburnum Purple leaf plum *Acer hersii* *Acer ginnala*	Camellia Sumach Lilac Berberis Mexican orange Laurustinus Laurel Rhododendron	*Helichrysum lanatum* Dwarf rhododendrons Rue Cotton lavender Daphne Spanish gorse
	Lombardy poplar Dawyck beech Cypress Douglas fir Incense cedar *Eucryphia* 'Nymansay'	Sweet bay *Prunus serrulata erecta* Certain cypress, e.g. *Chamaecyparis fletcheri* Irish yew *Prunus hillieri* 'Spire'	*Chamaecyparis lawsoniana* 'Ellwoodii' *Picea albertiana conica* *Crataegus monogyna stricta* *Viburnum farreri*	Dwarf juniper *Thuja* 'Rheingold' *Thuja plicata rogersii* *Berberis thunbergii* 'Erecta'
	Weeping willow Weeping ash Weeping beech Swedish birch	Young's weeping birch Weeping pear *Buddleia alternifolia* Weeping cherry Weeping ash	*Cotoneaster multiflorus* *Cotoneaster* 'Hybridus Pendulus' *Cotoneaster dielsianus* *Escallonia langleyensis*	*Viburnum davidii* *Juniperus depressa aurea* Dwarf weeping cedar *Cotoneaster conspicuus*
	Cedar of Lebanon ⎫ Scots pine ⎬ mature Austrian pine ⎭	*Prunus serrulata* Prunus 'Shiro-fugen' Cockspur thorn Dovaston yew	*Viburnum tomentosum mariesii* *Acer palmatum* 'Dissectum' *Lonicera pileata* *Pyracantha angustifolia*	*Cotoneaster horizontalis* *Cotoneaster microphyllus* *Cytisus kewensis* Prostrate juniper *Chaenomeles* 'Simonii'

	Maidenhair tree (*Ginkgo biloba*)
	Scots pine (*Pinus sylvestris*)
	Austrian pine (*Pinus nigra*)
	Mock acacia
	  (*Robinia pseudo-acacia*)
	Liquidambar styraciflua
	Tulip tree
	  (*Liriodendron tulipifera*)
	Monkey puzzle
	  (*Araucaria araucana*)
		Magnolia × soulangiana
		Parrotia persica
		Mt Etna broom
		Strawberry tree
		Autumn cherry
		Japanese maples
		Prunus serrula tibetica
		Acer griseum
			Rhus typhina
			Cytisus battandieri
			Clerodendron trichotomum
			Corylus avellana 'Contorta'
				Pernettya
				Miniature conifers
				Japanese azaleas
				Anchor plant
				  (*Colletia cruciata*)
				Teucrium fruticans

Yew hedge and archway, and a mature *Acer palmatum* 'Dissectum' used as a standard and shown here in its autumnal colouring.

Sheffield Park: a beautiful grouping of trees of different shape and foliage colour.

house; for these reasons we must talk of size in somewhat fluid terms, using an average small house as a yardstick.

The whole range might be covered in four groups ranging from zero to maximum:

1 Dwarf: up to about 1m (3ft) or ground-floor window-sill.
2 Small: up to bedroom windows, about 3·5m (12ft).
3 Medium: to roof height, above 9–12m (30–40ft).
4 Large: anything above roof height.

This way of considering plants as structural material with character, different in shape and in a range of sizes, is summarized in the table (page 109) which contains examples only. It will be appreciated that to make a complete reference chart would take the space of a good catalogue, especially if allowance were made for variations in normal and seasonal foliage colour, berry, flower colour, time of flowering and so on. Common names are used as far as possible and cross reference to a work on trees and shrubs and a visit to a nursery or park will help in selecting a plant for a particular position.

Clematis Jackmannii providing plant drapery.

The use of trees from the 'large' group will be restricted and depends on the size of the plot and its setting. For instance, it would be a mistake to plant a beech in a narrow plot hemmed in on all sides by neighbours, and yet one at the end of a garden backed by open country or waste land might be feasible. In the small garden, it pays to steer clear of possible trouble by using trees from the group of 'medium' growers.

PLANTING: SELECTION AND ARRANGEMENT

Thinking on the lines suggested, you will have now formed certain ideas and preferences; here you want a belt of plants for screening, or an individual tree for shade, there a carpet of low plants with something decorative rising from them, a sentinel to mark an important point, an internal division with a splash of colour facing the house, and so on. You will know roughly the shape and size of the planting needed for a particular position and are left with the problem of choice, spacing, and arrangement, which is a most satisfying part of garden-making.

Your thoughts will turn to flowering shrubs and trees and the array of colour they give. Though one can have something in flower at all seasons, the main show of blossom will be in the spring and early summer and one must remember that this is for a comparatively short time, while the form of the plants is always in evidence.

During the period when many of the shrubs have finished flowering, however, shrub and old-fashioned and floribunda roses can take over, later to be supported by such shrubs as flower in late summer and early

autumn, e.g. hibiscus, hoheria, ceanothus, buddleia, ceratostigma, hypericum, etc. The midsummer period is also the time when bold grouping of herbaceous plants among the shrubs will be the main attraction.

As the year advances, there will be the autumn foliage and the breaking of such plants as the winter-flowering cherry (*Prunus subhirtella* 'Autumnalis'), winter jasmine, wintersweet, and the winter-flowering viburnums.

The first essential is a good nursery catalogue, containing condensed information as to size, spread, foliage, flowering time, and so on, and when you appreciate the wide range of plants available you realize that the number of ways in which they can be arranged is infinite. Mark first the plants you know and like and those which from their description seem desirable. Then see as many as you can in your park or botanic garden or, better still, go to the nursery and talk to the grower. No good nursery will supply a plant merely to make a sale; if what you like is unsuitable to your soil and conditions they will suggest something else.

Make an enlarged rough plan of each planting area on a sheet of squared paper; use a scale which will allow you to write legibly. Useful metric scales are 1:50 (2cm to 1m), 1:100 (1cm to 1m), and 1:200 (5mm to 1m). A common imperial scale is $\frac{1}{4}$in to 1ft (1:48). On your graph paper mark positions for any medium-size trees which, unless they are the same, should not be closer than 5·5m (18ft). If you have room for more than two, avoid placing them in a straight line.

In the small garden with fences and neighbours to hide, you will need a core of evergreens. Tentatively mark these on your plan so that you have a fairly even distribution.

These will be dominant, particularly in the winter, and you will re-member the general silhouette and place the bigger growers (as given in the catalogue or from notes made at the nursery) where you want height and vice versa. Plants for this skeleton would include many of the berberis such as *B. stenophylla* and *B. darwinii*, certain cotoneasters which are almost evergreen, e.g. *C.* 'Watereri', arbutus, bay, choisya, cistus, elaeagnus, escal-lonia, garrya, holly, mahonia, myrtle, olearia, *Osmanthus × burkwoodii*, pittosporum, senecio, skimmia, stranvaesia, veronica, certain vibur-nums and, in lime-free soils, rhodo-dendron, camellia, kalmia and pernet-tya. These are just a few worth investigating.

Many of these evergreens have con-spicuous flowers and the colour and time of flowering can be noted on the plan. Do not let the evergreens form a solid wall, but bring some of the less vigorous, such as osmarea, *Berberis darwinii* and *Cotoneaster franchetii*, forward a little. Do not try to use too many kinds in a confined space or the effect will be restless; rather increase the number by making a group of three *Berberis stenophylla* about a metre (3ft) apart producing what will in time appear to be one enormous plant.

Among your evergreens space out the deciduous shrubs, keeping an eye on aspect so that those which like the sun are not in permanent shade, and planting near your trees subjects which will not mind the canopy: for example flowering currant, forsythia, pyracan-tha, mahonia, snowberry and St John's Wort (*Hypericum calycinum*).

SPACING

Your catalogue, or your own observa-tion, will tell you that a certain shrub can be expected to develop a width or spread of 2·5m (8ft). This can only be a rough guide, but it means that another shrub of similar stature can-not be closer than 2·5m (8ft). A border planted on these lines would be very sparse for some years and the shrubs would lack the mutual protection afforded by closer spacing. One should therefore arrange one's best, and pos-sibly more expensive, shrubs so that they will have room to develop with-out cramping each other, and to use cheaper expendable shrubs and her-baceous plants as filling.

As an alternative, where space per-mits, one could draw three lilacs to-gether spaced 1·25m (4ft) apart to give a bolder effect, but leave 2·5–3m (8–10ft) between the outside plant of this trio and a neighbour of similar size, again filling in between with smaller or expendable plants. Many of the small shrubs such as potentilla, cera-tostigma and cotton lavender look their best in drifts, planted 60cm (2ft) or so apart to form a billowing irregu-lar shape of foliage and flower round the base of a single larger-growing specimen. All the time keep in mind the shape of the plant and its foliage; contrast a small or finely divided leaf with an oval, an upright grower with one which droops, and spike-like growth with one of a softly rounded outline. Keep an eye on permanent or seasonal leaf colour so that interesting combinations of red leaf and grey, deep green and variegated, and so on, can be arranged. Remember the simple fact that to be of use to the colour arranger flowering periods must coincide or at least overlap.

DENSITY OF PLANTING

The cost of a shrub border will natur-ally vary with its role, and the kind of plants used. An average border (if

Shrubs planted for contrast of
shape and foliage.

there is such a thing), using groups of
small plants 60–90cm (2–3ft) apart,
some bigger growers about 1·25m
(4ft) apart, and a few specimens 2·5–
3m (8–10ft) apart, will take three
plants to every 4sq m (5sq yd) of
ground. If, when you have done your
layout plan, your density is greater
than this you are on the extravagant
side, and you can check and drop one
here and there from certain groups.

Once satisfied with the density,
send or take your list of plants to a
nursery, or nurseries. You will often
find quite a difference in prices, but
the important point is to go to a
nursery with a reputation for quality
and reliability.

For herbaceous plants, allow five to
the square metre (four to the square
yard); allow 60cm (2ft) spacing for
roses.

Apart from added interest, it is possible to economise by home propaga-
tion, accepting gifts from friends and,
where a nursery offers plants in varying sizes, by taking the smallest. It is
false economy to go in for 'cheap'
offers which you are unable to see, or
to buy enormous plants from land
clearance at cheap rates, unless such
offers are made by a reputable nursery. As a general practice stick to
small plants. They are safe and sure
and the inevitable odd loss is not an
expensive one.

7 SOME USEFUL TREES FOR LITTLE GARDENS

Having become interested in gardening one soon learns that all plants do not grow with equal facility. Each thrives in conditions which suit it best. Most of our garden plants originally came from widely separated parts of the earth, from North America to Europe, China to Chile, and to provide even the approximate climate and environment of their natural habitat all in one place presents a great problem. Even within the British Isles there are differences – more between east and west than north and south – which can make a plant grow well on the west coast of Scotland and yet fail on the drier east side.

Obviously, no plant can be expected to grow if it is maltreated – though some will battle on when according to all the rules they should be dead – but there are a great many that are not too fastidious. These are the stalwarts which will serve the new gardener. The list is long and varied and the selection here is inevitably one of personal choice. Many are quite common but none the less desirable.

It is not easy to draw the line between trees which can be used in a

Betula pendula 'Youngii' in autumn colour.

small garden and those which should not. Of the forest trees listed on page 109 some, though tall, are slender or not of great bulk, such as the cypress *Chamaecyparis lawsoniana* 'Columnaris' or the Dawyck beech which reaches upwards and takes about twenty years to attain 12m (40ft) and is then only 3.5m (12ft) or so through. Birches may also find their way into a little garden since they are delicate enough not to be overpowering. Some forest trees may also be suitable in small rural plots backing onto open country; even in built-up areas neighbours with long narrow strips might by mutual agreement plant larger trees at the farther end to form their own communal bit of woodland.

If one had to make a rule, however, it would be that trees such as are exemplified in column one of the list on page 109 are unsuitable for the *small* individual plot. They are material for wider landscape application, those which the planner uses to settle a *cluster* of houses into its surroundings.

This unfortunately rules out trees for which so many people ask – the ever popular copper beech and weeping willow – but there are substitutes as will be seen below:

ROUNDED OUTLINE

Name and origin	*notes*
Acer campestre (Common maple) native	A good 'country' tree. Amber autumn colour.
A. ginnala (Maple) China and Japan	A small tree from the big family of maples. About 6m (20ft). Small yellowish white, fragrant flowers in May; brilliant autumn colour.
A. negundo 'Variegatum' France, but species is North American	Striking variegated foliage especially with dark background.
Amelanchier lamarckii (The Snowy Mespilus or June Berry) North America and Canada	Graceful small tree or big shrub. Sheeted with white flowers mid-April for about a week. Rich autumn colour.
Cornus mas (Cornelian Cherry) Europe	A large shrub or spreading tree of about 6m (20ft). Yellow flowers on the bare wood end of February. Red berries.
Cotoneaster North Asia	This big genus provides a wealth of garden shrubs, some of which can be trained to a single stem or leader to form a handsome tree, ideal for screening.
C. 'Cornubia' *C.* 'Watereri'.	Evergreen or nearly so; fronding, long narrow leaves; crop of brilliant red berries.

C. lacteus	Leaves oval and white underneath; retains its berry well.
Crataegus oxycantha (Thorn) Native	The Hawthorn or May. Double white, pink or red flowers.
C. × lavallei: 'Carrierei' uncertain origin	White flowers June, large orange red fruit; large oval leaves stay green late in the year; dense head.
C. prunifolia uncertain origin: possibly a hybrid	Wider than high; rich red fruit and brilliant autumn colour.
Laburnum anagyroides Europe	Well-known tree flowering in May and early June; yellow flowers. The variety 'Aureum' has yellow leaves, too.
L. alpinum (Scotch Laburnum)	Sturdy tree; longer racemes of flower in June.
L. × watereri 'Vossii'	A fine form with very long flower racemes in June.
Malus (Crab)	A great family of popular trees of which the following few are representative.
M. floribunda	Broad headed, twiggy, and arching; flowers pale pink and crimson end of April.
M. 'Golden Hornet'	White flowers; bright yellow fruits until late in the year: one of the best.
M. hupehensis	Use when a white blossom is needed; fragrant flower in June.
M. 'John Downie'	A good fruiting crab; a fine sight of yellow and scarlet. Flower is white in early May.
M. 'Profusion'	Large wine red flowers in clusters end of April and early May. Young foliage is red tinted. A similar variety is *M.* 'Lemoinei'.
M. 'Red Sentinel'	White flowers; deep red fruits throughout the winter.
M. × robusta (A Siberian crab)	Another with white flower and fine scarlet fruit which hangs until February.
Prunus (Plum, Almond, Peach, Cherry)	This enormous family gives us a great wealth of spring colour. They should be seen when selecting though one can scarcely go wrong. The following should be considered:
P. × blireana (Plum) Europe and North-West Asia	The much admired double pink blossom on bare wood in March; foliage is copper. A small tree, say 4·5–5·5m (15–18ft).

Prunus serrula in a London
front garden.

P. cerasifera 'Pissardii' Persia	Another well-known red foliage tree which in the small garden can be used as substitute for copper beech. Delicate pink blossom in March.
P. dulcis (Almond) South Europe and West Asia	Delicate pink blossom on bare wood in March. Likes a warm well drained soil and shows best against a dark background.
P. persica (Peach) China	Suitable in warmer parts of the country and in a sheltered position. Double deep pink flowers in April. As a preventive against leaf curl peaches and almonds need a spray of lime sulphur before bud burst.

P. cerasus (Cherry)	Six are suggested below to give variety of colour and to spread out the flowering period:
P. incisa Fuji cherry Japan	A small tree for restricted space; masses of pink buds opening to white in late March.
P. 'Tai-Haku'	Large white flowers with slightly bronzed foliage. Makes a spreading tree and is more often free of bird damage than most other cultivars of cherry.
P. 'Pink Perfection'	Large double pink flowers in profusion end of April early May.
P. padus (Bird Cherry) Native	Racemes of small white fragrant flowers which are grouped along a centre stem (rather like buddleia) in May.
P. serrulata 'Shimidsu'	Clusters of pure white double flowers (pink in the bud) hang from the branches at end of April and in early May. Growth horizontal in older trees.
P. subhirtella 'Autumnalis' (Winter Flowering Cherry) Japan	A wide-spreading though graceful tree which has the virtue of flowering during mild spells all through the winter. 'Autumnalis Rosea' has a pink flower.
Sorbus aria (Whitebeam) Native	When the small garden needs a 'large' tree, remember this sturdy native which does well on most soils and is particularly at home on chalk.
S. aria 'Lutescens'	Leaves are downy and a soft 'pastel' green, especially when unfolding. Both have white 'felt' on underside of leaves which with the white flower makes the tree a fine sight in spring.
S. aria 'Majestica'	Large green leaves; white flower in May and red fruit.
S. aucuparia (Mountain Ash or Rowan)	A well-known tree admirable for the fernlike appearance of its foliage, its white flower in May and its masses of scarlet fruit in September.
S. discolor China	Similar tree, not so good in flower and fruit but with splendid autumn colour.
S. hupehensis China	The berries are white tinted with pink.

A FEW FASTIGIATE OR ERECT-BRANCHED TREES

Name and origin	*notes*
Carpinus betulus 'Fastigiata' (Fastigiate hornbeam) Europe	Better than beech on heavy soil, but will become broad with age.
Chamaecyparis lawsoniana 'Allumii' (Lawson's cypress) Western North America	This 'blue' conifer is popular and readily obtainable, but care should be used in its placing as it can grow to 12m (40ft) or more. Too often used in the young state as ornament near windows where it can become a nuisance.
C.l. 'Columnaris'	A dense narrow column of 'blue' which makes a fine specimen of architectural character.
C.l. 'Erecta Viridis'	Raised in England, a pointed pyramid of bright green. With age it is inclined to become brown and bare at the base and best used where it can be fronted with shrubs.
C. l. 'Fletcheri'	A better conifer for the small garden. Slow growth takes many years to reach 3·5m (12ft). Beautifully feathery, bluish-grey.
C. l. 'Lutea'	Where a golden cypress is required. A pale golden yellow in colour. The cultivar 'Stewartii' is a good alternative.
Crataegus monogyna stricta (Common thorn) Native	A tough little tree for a confined space.
Fagus sylvatica 'Dawyck' (Dawyck Beech) Native	A spire-like tree useful in association with tall buildings even in confined spaces.
Juniperus virginiana 'Skyrocket'	One of the narrowest of all conifers; foliage blue grey; fairly fast grower; 1·5–2m × 30cm (5–7ft × 1ft).
Prunus 'Amanogawa' (Cherry) Japan	Pale pink, fragrant double flowers; branches grow almost vertically.
P. hillieri 'Spire'	Raised in England, a slender tree somewhat bigger than the above.

Taxus baccata 'Fastigiata' (The Irish Yew) Native	The well known Yew of the Churchyard. Erect and upreaching but with age can become broad. 'Fastigiata Aurea' has golden young leaves.

SOME MEDIUM SIZED TREES OF WEEPING HABIT

Name and origin	*notes*
Betula pendula 'Youngii' (Young's weeping birch) Native	A perfect weeping tree for the small lawn.
Buddleia alternifolia	A large shrub which can be trained as a small tree; the long arching branches resemble those of a miniature weeping willow with fragrant lilac-coloured flowers in June.
Prunus serrulata 'Cheal's Weeping'	A good example of the weeping cherry. Deep pink double flowers in late April and early May.
Pyrus salicifolia 'Pendula' (Weeping pear) South-east Europe	The white flower and fruit are of little consequence. The attraction lies in the soft silver green willow-like foliage on pendulous branches.
Salix caprea pendula (Kilmarnock Willow)	The weeping form of 'pussy willow'; it reaches a height of 3m (10ft).

TREES WITH A TENDENCY TO HORIZONTAL OUTLINE

Name and origin	*notes*
Crataegus crus-galli (The Cockspur thorn) East North America	A flattish-headed tree with enormous spines; white flower in June and large deep red fruit which persist. The autumn colour is brilliant.
Prunus serrulata (Japanese Cherry) China	The original Japanese Cherry with low wide-spreading branches. Double pure white flowers at the end of April. *P. serrulata* 'Alborosea' or 'Shirofugen' has white flowers pink in the bud and opening with the young pinkish bronze foliage. A fine low tree, but needs room to spread sideways.

TREES WITH SPECIAL DECORATIVE CHARACTERISTICS

These are many and varied and can be used in special points of interest in the garden. A few for example would be:

Name and origin	notes
Arbutus unedo (Strawberry tree) Mediterranean regions and south-west Ireland	An evergreen with dark green leathery leaves. Drooping panicles of pinkish bell-shaped flowers in late autumn at the same time as the strawberrylike fruit. Does not mind lime soil, but is always best started small from a pot and needs some shelter.
Cotinus obovatus	A large shrub or small tree, formerly called *Rhus cotinoides*. Oval leaves which colour brilliantly in autumn.
Parrotia persica North Persia	The feature of this fine deciduous tree is the foliage in autumn. The 12cm (5in) oval leaves provide a wonderful variety of colour, gold slashed with scarlet to deep crimson.
Prunus serrula (Tibetica)	Worth a place in the garden for the beauty of its mahogany red bark which peels to reveal a highly 'polished' copper colour beneath.
Rhus typhina (Sumach) East North America	A wide-headed, small tree with large, pinnate leaves which colour well in autumn. Even when bare the soft branches make interesting patterns.
R. typhina laciniata	The foliage is deeply feathered and turns orange and yellow in autumn.

8 GOOD-NATURED SHRUBS FOR BEGINNERS

When selecting shrubs, you will naturally choose those which you and your family like, but with the design as a whole in mind and, being practical, you will need to watch the following points: (a) Soil; (b) Aspect; (c) Climate; (d) Shape, size and general character; (e) Texture of foliage; (f) Colour of foliage and flower; (g) Cost. The order is important, since it is no use satisfying (d) to (g) if the plant will not grow anyway.

Consider first your soil which is likely to be the greatest limiting factor and can vary physically and chemically within a radius of a mile or so. It may be sandy, gravelly, of relatively coarse texture (a term which applied to soil refers to the size of the particles) or at the other extreme the fine homogeneous particles characteristic of clay. Soil also has a quality called structure, which, as its name implies, is its organization: the particles, themselves inert mineral, being 'laced' by a framework of fine organic matter to give a substance which, when handled, does not trickle through the fingers or compress into a solid mass, but crumbles.

Such soil, full of vegetable matter, is 'alive' and in the presence of air, moisture and lime, is subject to the action of beneficial bacteria which release essential plant foods. There may be so much lime in the soil that it has a strong alkaline reaction and in some limestone districts it can, of course, be seen. On the other hand, a deficiency of lime inhibits bacterial action and the vegetable content is only partially decomposed. Such soil is peat or the kind of brown fluffy mould where one finds bracken growing. Half-way between these two extremes, of course, we have a neutral soil.

There is a whole group of plants, containing such subjects as rhododendron, azalea, kalmia, pieris, summer-flowering heathers and others, which just do not tolerate lime, and it is a waste of money to buy them unless the soil is suitable. It is much better to reconcile yourself to being without and concentrate on the host of good plants which *will* grow for you.

Soil structure can be improved by the addition of humus in the form of manure, leaf mould, compost, spent hops, or peat, all of which have a normalizing effect making poor sand into a better moisture-holding medium and helping clay to break up and become more friable. This latter process is also assisted by the addition of grit or course sand.

All this, however, takes time and, if you should be on land which needs improvement, it is wise to start with plants which are not too fastidious.

In the following select list, evergreens are indicated by an asterisk (*). Beneath each plant name are given in Roman figures the months when the plant is at its best; in most cases this signifies the flowering period, but where fruiting is a feature this is stated below the figures denoting the relevant months. In a few cases where the foliage is of interest for most of the year no months of interest are given.

The figures under 'height' and 'radius' represent ten-year development and should be regarded as very approximate since they are subject to environment. 'Radius' represents the rough measurement from stem to edge of spread. This added to the figure for a selected neighbour gives a guide as to spacing. Where plants are to be grouped to make a drift or block they can be closer.

SHRUBS EVENTUALLY REACHING ABOVE EYE LEVEL

Name and season of interest	height metres (feet)	radius metres (feet)	notes
BERBERIS			The Barberries are an enormous family which provide some fine deciduous and evergreen shrubs. They like sun but tolerate shade. Examples are:
B. darwinii* IV–V, X–XII (fruits)	2·5 + (8 +)	1–1·25 (3–4)	Small deep green glossy leaves lightly spined. Rich orange yellow flower, blue berries in autumn.
B. stenophylla* V	2·5 (8)	1·5 (5)	Deep green small narrow leaves on slender arching stems. Builds up to a dense shrub, a waterfall of golden flower in spring and a fine background plant after. Blue round berries.
BUDDLEIA davidii VII–IX	2·75–3·5 (9–12)	1·5–2 (5–6)	The well-known haunt of butterflies. Many magnificent cultivars. 'Black Knight' (deep violet), 'Fascination' (lilac pink), 'Royal Red' (red purple) and 'White Cloud' are examples.
CHAENOMELES (CYDONIA) III–IV			Also known as Quince and Japonica. Apart from its value as a wall plant it makes a shrub in the open and will stand shade.
C. 'Crimson and Gold'	1–1·5 (3–5)	1 (3)	A dense hummock with crimson petals and golden anthers.

C. 'Knap Hill Scarlet'	2 (6)	1 (3)	Orange-scarlet, wax-like flowers.
C. 'Moerloosii'	2–2·5 (6–8)	1 (3)	Arching and spreading. Flowers white tinted pink on outside.
C. 'Pink lady'	1·25 (4)	1·5 (5)	Spreading habit; flowers clear rose pink.
CORNUS IX–XII, I–III (winter bark)			The Dogwoods are many. In this group the flower and berry are of less consequence than the handsome foliage and winter bark.
C. *alba* 'Sibirica'	1·5 (5)	1·5 (5)	The scarlet bark is particularly pleasing in winter sunshine.
C. *alba* 'Spaethii'	2 (6)	1 (3)	Golden variegation.
C. *alba* 'Variegata'	2 (6)	1·25 (4)	Leaves margined creamy white; a valuable variegated shrub.
C. *stolonifera* 'Flaviramea'	2 (6)	1·25 (4)	Creamy yellow bark.
CORYLUS MAXIMA 'Purpurea'	3·25 + (10 +)	1·5 (5)	The rich brown purple foliage of this well-shaped plant is sufficient to commend it.
C. *avellana* 'Aurea'	2 (6)	2 (6)	A contrast to the above is the golden foliage of this cobnut.
COTINUS *coggygria* VI–VII	3 (9)	1 (3)	Formerly called *Rhus cotinus*. Smooth rounded green leaves; gives good autumn colour. Fawn pink plume-like inflorescence smothers the plant in summer.
C. *c.* 'Foliis Purpureis' VI–X	2 (6)	1 (3)	Rich purple foliage which colours red in the autumn; pink inflorescence in summer.
C. *c. purpureus*	2 (6)	1 (3)	Green leaves turn yellow; inflorescence like pink smoke.
COTONEASTER VI–VII, IX–XII (fruits)			Another big genus which provides shrubs for foliage and form effects. Hawthorn-like flower. Notable for fine crops of berry in autumn.

Cotinus coggyria 'Foliis Purpureis', with a white shrub rose, golden privet behind and in the foreground massed *Hypericum calycinum*.

C. 'Cornubia'	3·5 (12)	3·25 (10)	Fast-growing semi-evergreens with heavy crops of red berries invaluable for providing height and for screening; tolerate shade.
C. 'St Monica'	3·5 + (12 +)	2·5 (8)	
C. *franchetii**	3·25 (10)	1·5 (5)	Graceful arching growth; grey-green leaves, orange-scarlet berries.
C. 'Hybridus Pendulus'	2·75 (9)	1 (3)	Grafted on a 2m (6ft) stem forms a cascade of red berries in winter.
C. *lacteus**	3·5–4·5 (12–15)	1·5 (5)	Oval leaves white on underside; dark red berries persist through the winter.

C. salicifolius* floccosus	3·25 (10)	1·5 (5)	Arching habit with narrow leaves; small red berries.
C. simonsii	2·5 (8)	1–1·25 (3–4)	Semi-evergreen, erect growth, brilliant scarlet berries.
CYTISUS (Broom)			Though the typical broom has a generally softly rounded outline, the characteristic brush-like structure makes it an excellent foil to broad-leaved plants. One cannot assume that it will grow anywhere because some do not like lime.
C. albus (Portugal Broom)	2 (6)	1 (3)	A handsome plant with delicate stems and grey-green foliage, particularly good when there is space for a group. Masses of white flower in May.
C. battandieri VI–VII	4 (13)	2·5 (8)	Unlike the type, it resembles laburnum. The leaves are a silky silver-green and the flowers like the tip of a lupin, bright yellow and pineapple-scented. A fine wall plant, but makes a shrub in the open.
DEUTZIA scabra 'Flore Pleno' VI–VII	3·25 (10)	1 (3)	Double white flowers flushed outside with a purple tint. The plant is erect and vase-shaped; stands some shade. The variety 'Candidissima' is pure white.
ELAEAGNUS* × ebbingei	3·25 (10)	1·25–1·5 (4–5)	A handsome plant with grey-green glossy leaves. Useful for shelter and background.
EUONYMUS alatus IX–XII (fruits)	2·25 (7)	1·25 (4)	A slow grower but decorative. The bark develops corky 'wings' and the 'Purple' fruit is showy; the foliage turns a rosy scarlet.
E. europaeus IX–XII (fruits)	3·25 (10)	1·25 (4)	A background plant or small tree; the native Spindle is noted for its red- and orange-coloured fruit.

FORSYTHIA × *intermedia* 'Lynwood' III	2·5 + (8 +)	1·5 (5)	A very good wide-flowered form of the well-known spring shrub.
GENISTA *tenera* VI–VII	3·5 (12)	2 (6)	The Madeira Broom. Soft grey-green brush-like form with masses of brilliant yellow flowers. Stands shade.
HYDRANGEA *paniculata* 'Grandiflora' VIII	2 (6)	1 (3)	Handsome panicles of creamy white flowers which fade to a pink. Arching habit.
KERRIA *japonica* 'Pleniflora' V–VI	2·5 (8)	1 (3)	Upright and arching. Bright green foliage and double orange yellow flowers.
LIGUSTRUM* *japonicum* VII–IX	1·25 (4)	1 (3)	A handsome privet with large panicles of white flower.
L. lucidum 'Tricolor'	2 (6)	1·5 (5)	Narrow leaves with irregular white border tinged pink when young.
OSMANTHUS × *burkwoodii** IV	2·5 (8)	1·25 (4)	A fine plant, compact and dense with olive-green oval leaves and tiny white tubular flowers which are scented. A slow grower to full stature.
PHILADELPHUS VII			There is a wide choice.
P. 'Belle Etoile'	1·5 (5)	1 (3)	Sweetly scented, single white flowers, pink at base.
P. 'Burfordiensis'	3·25 (10)	1 (3)	Single, cup-shaped pink-based flowers with yellow stamens.
P. coronarius			A strong grower with small creamy flowers with the typical powerful scent.
P. 'Virginal'	2·5 (8)	1·25 (4)	Fragrant double white upright.

PHOTINA × *fraseri* 'Red Robin'	2 (6)	1 (3)	Brilliant red young foliage.
RIBES *sanguineum* III–IV	3 (9)	1 (3)	The common but none the less attractive flowering currant with deep crimson flowers.
R. *sanguineum* 'Pulborough Scarlet'	2–2·25 (6–7)	1 (3)	Crimson flower.
ROSA			The shrub roses are many and varied and should be seen. Of the bigger growers the following are noteworthy:
R. *chinensis* 'Sophie's Perpetual'	1·25 (4)	1·25 (4)	Deep crimson buds, opening to pink cup-shaped flowers, scented.
R. 'Frühlingsgold' V–VI	2·5 (8)	2 (6)	Semi-double, pale yellow, scented.
R. *moyesii* 'Geranium' VI, IX–X (fruits)	2·5–3·25 (8–10)	1·5 (5)	Arching open growth; red single flowers and fine red bottle-shaped fruit.
R. 'Nevada' VI, IX	2–2·5 (6–8)	1·25–1·5 (4–5)	Arching growth. Large single flowers white-tinted pink; recurrent flowering.
R. *rubrifolia* VI	2·25–2·5 (7–8)	1·5 (5)	Stems and underside of leaves a purplish red. Upper surfaces of leaves have the appearance of a grey-green bloom; flowers dainty, pink with white centre and yellow stamens. Hips later are purple.
R. *rugosa* 'Blanc Double de Coubert' VI	2–2·5 (6–8)	1·25–1·5 (4–5)	Crinkled bright green leaves; semi-double white frilled flowers. Scented.
R. *xanthina spontanea* ('Canarybird') V	2·5 (8)	1·5 (5)	A great favourite. Handsome foliage on golden arching stems; covered with single yellow flowers.
RUBUS × *tridel* 'Benenden' V–VI	2–2·5 (6–8)	1·5 (5)	This 'Bramble' has large saucer-shaped white flowers with yellow stamens carried singly all along the arching branches.

SAMBUCUS *racemosa* 'Plumosa Aurea'	2·5 (8)	2 (6)	Slow-growing, yet valuable not only for its white flower and red berries in spring and summer but for its finely cut golden foliage.
SORBARIA *aitchisonii* VII–VIII	2·75 (9)	1·5 (5)	Fronding brown stems with fern-like foliage. Panicles of pure white flower. An elegant form plant.
SPARTIUM *junceum* VII–VIII	2·5 (8)	1 (3)	Spanish Broom. Erect brush-like growth loaded with scented, yellow 'pea' flowers in late summer.
SPIRAEA 'Arguta' IV–V	2–2·5 (6–8)	1·25 (4)	A dainty plant foaming with white spring flowers.
S. × *vanhouttei* V–VI	2·5 (8)	1·25 (4)	Arching branches with attractive foliage and white flower to follow S. 'Arguta'.
SYMPHORICARPUS VI–VII, X–XII (fruits)			Snowberry. The flower is pretty but small and inconspicuous. Apart from that this plant has many virtues. Shapely, and with foliage which can be cut for decoration it thrives in shade under trees and in October is laden with glistening berries which persist through the winter. Though deciduous it is so twiggy it makes an effective screen.
S. *albus laevigatus*	2·5 (8)	spreads	Pure white berry.
S. 'Magic Berry'			Pink berry.
S. *orbiculatus*			Pink berry.
S. 'White Hedge'			Compact and upright growth; small white berry.
SYRINGA (Lilac) V–VI			
S. × *josiflexa* 'Bellicent'	3·25 + (10 +)	1·5 (5)	A Canadian hybrid; tall panicles of rose-coloured flowers like gigantic privet.
S. × *persica*	2 (6)	1·25 (4)	Persian lilac. A much daintier plant than the others mentioned; lavender-coloured scented flowers.

S. × *persica* 'Alba'	2 (6)	1·25 (4)	White flower.
S. vulgaris	3·5 + (12 +)	1·5 (5)	Choice of lilacs must be a personal one, but from a long list these are popular.
S. 'Firmament'			Blue single, buds mauve.
S. 'Katherine Havemeyer'			Heavy-headed double purple lavender.
S. 'Mme Lemoine'			A well known double white.
S. 'Mrs Edward Harding'			Double red-tinted pink.
S. 'Primrose'			Primrose single.
S. 'Souvenir de Louis Spath'			Single dark red.
S. 'Vestale'			A fine single white.
VIBURNUM			
V. × *bodnantense* XII–II	2·75 + (9 +)	1·5 (5)	Representative of the winter-flowering viburnums. Rose-flushed fragrant flowers on the bare wood. Others are *V. farreri*, *V. grandiflorum* (its parents), *V.* 'Candidissima' which is pure white, and 'Deben', pink flowers opening to white.
V. 'Deben' XI–IV	3 (10)	1·25 (4)	
V. × *burkwoodii** IV	2·5–3·25 (8–10)	1·5 (5)	A semi-evergreen with dark green oval leaves and rounded heads of fragrant white flowers.
V. plicatum tomentosum 'Lanarth' *V. p. t.* 'Mariesii' V	2·75 + (9 +)	2 (6)	'Lanarth' and 'Mariesii' both reach out horizontally decked with flat white flowers.
V. opulus V–VI	3·25–4·5 (10–15)	2–2·25 (6–7)	Our native Guelder Rose with flat scented white flowers followed by clusters of translucent red berries. Good autumn foliage colour.
V. opulus 'Roseum' V–VI	3·25–4·5 (10–15)	2–2·25 (6–7)	An old favourite, the Snowball tree; yellowish green flower developing to white.

WEIGELA
(Diervilla)
V–VI

W.'Abel Carriere'	2 (6)	2 (6)	Rosy carmine flowers with a pink throat.
W. 'Bristol Ruby'	2–2·5 (6–8)	1·25 (4)	An arching shrub with rich red trumpet flowers.

SHRUBS AT EYE-LEVEL OR BELOW

Name and season of interest	height metres (feet)	radius metres (feet)	notes
BERBERIS *B. × carminea* 'Barbarossa'	2 (6)	1·25 (4)	Masses of translucent berries turning scarlet with richly coloured autumn foliage.
B. × stenophylla 'Coccinea'*	1 (3)	0·45 (1½)	Small dark green leaves, coral flowers, compact.
B. thunbergii III–IV, IX–XI (fruits + foliage)	1·5 (5)	1·25 (4)	Fresh green foliage turning to brilliant autumn tints with scarlet berries. Height variable.
B. thunbergii atropurpurea	2 (6)	1·25 (4)	Purple foliage.
B. thunbergii 'Erecta'	1·5 (5)	0·3 (1)	Upright form.
B. wilsoniae	1–1·25 (3–4)	1·25 (4)	Wide spreading, small greyish green leaves; good autumn colour; coral fruit clusters.
BUDDLEIA *davidii* *nanhoensis* VII–X	2 (6)	1 (3)	A small buddleia with dainty clear mauve spikes of flower.
CERATOSTIGMA *willmottianum* (Plumbago) VII–X	1 (3)	0·45 (1½)	If cut down annually, it breaks again from the base. Bright clear blue flowers.
CHAENOMELES (Cydonia) III–IV *C. japonica*	1 (3)	1 (3)	Flowers bright orange.

C. 'Rowallane'	1·25 (4)	1·5 (5)	Spreading habit with crimson wax-like flowers.
C. 'Simonii'	0·75 (2½)	0·6 (2)	Semi-double crimson flowers.
COTONEASTER *horizontalis* V, IX–XII (fruits)	0·6–1·25 (2–4)	1·25–1·5 (4–5)	Low and sideways reaching. Herringbone formation. Rich autumn colour and red berries.
CYTISUS *nigricans* VII–VIII	1 (3)	0·6 (2)	A compact late broom with bright yellow flowers.
C. × *praecox* V	1·5 (5)	1 (3)	Arching growth, grey green foliage, cream flower.
C. *purgans* IV–VI	1·25 (4)	0·6 (2)	Grey-green rush-like growth. Fragrant golden yellow flowers.
DAPHNE *mezereum* II–III	1–1·25 (3–4)	0·6 (2)	This must be included for its purplish red, very fragrant flower on the bare wood at a time when most needed. The berry is red. There is a white form with orange berry.
DEUTZIA × *rosea* VI	1·25 (4)	1 (3)	Compact, arching branches; flower is bell-shaped and pink.
D. × *rosea* 'Campanulata'	1·25 (4)	1 (3)	A white form. A graceful plant.
ERICA *erigena* III–IV	1·25 (4)	0·45 (1½)	A bush heather tolerant of alkaline soil. Fragrant rose flowers. Best used in an informal setting.
E. *terminalis* (Corsican Heath) VI–XI	1–1·5 (3–5)	0·3–0·6 (1–2)	A lime-tolerant heath forming an erect bush bearing rose-coloured flowers which turn brown and remain. Flowering in late summer it can well be associated with earlier ones (see pages 138–9) to spread the interest.
GENISTA *hispanica* VI–VII	0·6 (2)	0·6 (2)	Spanish Gorse. A spiney cushion closely studded with bright yellow flowers. Excellent for banks and irregular drifts.

G. lydia V–VI	0·6–1 (2–3)	1–1·25 (3–4)	Another for banks; curving growth. Golden yellow flowers.
HYPERICUM × *inodorum* 'Elstead'	1 (3)	1 (3)	Brilliant salmon red fruits.
H. patulum* VII–X	1–1·25 (3–4)	0·6 (2)	Deep green leaves. A bushy plant with the rich yellow saucer flowers of the well-known St John's Wort and 5cm (2in) across. Colours in autumn.
H. 'Hidcote' VII–X	1·5 (5)	1 (3)	A similar plant but taller and with larger flowers.
LAVANDULA *angustifolia** VI–IX	1–1·25 (3–4)	0·6 (2)	Old English lavender.
L. spica 'Twickel Purple'*	0·6–1 (2–3)	0·45 (1½)	Neat and bushy; strong colour.
L. spica ''vera''*	0·6–1 (2–3)	0·45 (1½)	Dutch lavender; broad foliage.
MAHONIA *aquifolium** III–IV	1–1·25 (3–4)	0·6 (2)	A good carpeting plant useful under trees, but will grow 1·25m (4ft) high. Soft holly-like leaves; clusters of yellow flowers followed by purple-blue berries.
PHILADELPHUS VI–VII 'Manteau d'Hermine'	1–1·25 (3–4)	0·75 (2½)	A small philadelphus with scented creamy white, double flowers.
P. microphyllus	1·25 (4)	0·75 (2½)	Dainty twiggy little shrub with tiny sweetly scented white flowers.
P. 'Sybille'	1 (3)	0·5 (2)	Arching and bearing scented white flowers with purple centre.
POTENTILLA 'Abbotswood'	0·75 (2½)	1·5 (5)	Grey foliage and white flowers. A foil for a red foliage neighbour.
P. 'Elizabeth'	1 (3)	1·25 (4)	Bright green foliage; deep yellow flowers.
P. 'Katherine Dykes' V–IX	1·5 (5)	1 (3)	Bushy with primrose yellow flowers over a long period. Will tolerate some shade.

Opposite: clockwise from the top left, *Olearia nummulariifolia, Philadelphus* and *Viburnum davidii*, with *Stachys lanata* in the foreground.

RUTA *graveolens* (Rue)	0·6–0·9 (2–3)	0·45 (1½)	An aromatic plant with bluish foliage (especially in 'Jackman's Blue') and yellow flowers.
SENECIO Dunedin Hybrids*	1·25–1·5 (4–5)	0·5 (2)	Silver-grey oval leaves on a shrub which is inclined to straggle and sometimes best controlled. Yellow daisy-like flowers.
SKIMMIA *japonica** X–XII (fruits) S.'Foremanii'*	1–1·5 (3–5)	0·5 (2)	Roughly domed in shape with pleasing narrowly oval leaves and bearing scented white flowers; to ensure good crops of red berries, plant male and female varieties together. 'Foremanii' is a good female form. Fine plants for a shaded position.
S. *japonica* 'Rubella'	1·25 (4)		A good male form. Red buds in winter, opening in spring to white flowers.
SPIRAEA *japonica* 'Anthony Waterer' V	1–1·5 (3–5)	0·5 (2)	Attractive foliage with minor pink and cream variegations. Flat heads of rosy red flowers.
S. *japonica* 'Goldflame'	0·75 (2½)	0·75 (2½)	'Gold' foliage with crimson flowers in July.
VIBURNUM *carlesii* IV–V	1·25–1·5 (4–5)	1 (3)	Grey-green foliage and large rounded flower clusters white-flushed pink and strongly scented like carnations; worth growing for this alone.
VIBURNUM *davidii* (fruits)	0·75 (2½)	0·5 (2)	A low but dignified and handsome shrub which owes little to its dull white flower. Long oval leaves, dark green, each strongly marked by three veins. The plant reaches sideways rather than upwards. Male and female forms planted together ensure good blue oval fruit.
WEIGELA 'Newport Red' VII	1·25–1·5 (4–5)	0·75 (2½)	Arching growth and rich red trumpet flowers.
W. *florida* 'Variegata' VI	1·5 (5)	1·25 (4)	Creamy yellow variegated foliage, pale pink flowers.

Note on Roses
There are a great many Floribunda Roses, for example 'Lili Marlene' (dark red), 'Queen Elizabeth' (pink), 'Korona' (orange), 'City of Belfast' (red), 'Allgold' (yellow), and 'Iceberg' (white), which are invaluable for summer effect when grouped among shrubs.

Rose-lovers will find much of interest in the investigation of the 'old fashioned' roses and species. These are numerous and so varied in their appeal that it would be invidious to select and they should be seen.

SMALL SHRUBS

Name and season of interest	height centi-metres (feet	radius centi-metres (feet)	notes
BERBERIS × *stenophylla** 'Corallina Compacta'	45 (1½)	30 (1)	A shrublet with tiny leaves and coral buds opening to deep yellow.
B. *thunbergii* 'Atropurpurea Nana'	60 (2)	30 (1)	A miniature of the purple leaf Barberry; suitable for the rock garden.
BUXUS *sempervirens* 'Suffructicosa'*			Box edging beloved by so many people for its scent and associations.
COTONEASTER *congestus* X–XII (fruits)	30 (1)	—	A small dark-green-leaved creeping evergreen of hummock growth.
C. *dammeri** X–XII (fruits)			A prostrate evergreen clinging to the contours and sprinkled with red berries in autumn.
C. *microphyllus** *cochleatus* X–XII	15–30 (½–1)		Another horizontal growing evergreen with large red berries.
CYTISUS × *beanii* V	30 (1)	60 (2)	Semi-prostrate with sprays of golden yellow flowers.
C. × *kewensis* V–VI	40 (1¼)	60–90 (2–3)	A prostrate broom with cream flowers.
C. *procumbens* V–VI	5 (2in)	90 (3)	Clings to the ground; yellow flowers.

Hinton: Buxus sempervirens.

ERICA			Heathers can be included in a general list but with reservations. Only those shown will tolerate lime, and their well-being will depend on the soil being well prepared and on plenty of peat added at the time of planting.
E. × *darleyensis** XI–IV	45 ($1\frac{1}{2}$)	30 (1)	Soft purplish rose, bushy growth.
E. erigena* 'Brightness' III–V	45–60 ($1\frac{1}{2}$–2)	30 (1)	Rose pink, slow grower.
E. erigena* 'Silver Beads' III–V	45 ($1\frac{1}{2}$)	30 (1)	Compact shapely growth with white flowers.
E. herbacea *(carnea)*	30 (1)	25 ($\frac{3}{4}$)	Rosy flowers. There are many varieties all about the same in size except where noted.

E. h. 'Atrorubens' III–IV			Deep pink flower.
E. h. 'King George' XI–II			An earlier flowering cultivar.
E. h. 'Spring- wood Pink'* II–III	25 ($\frac{3}{4}$)	30 (1)	Clear rose pink.
E. h. 'Springwood White'* II–III	25 ($\frac{3}{4}$)	30 (1)	A fine white variety.
E. h. 'Vivelli' II–III	15 ($\frac{1}{2}$)	15 ($\frac{1}{2}$)	Deep carmine.
E. h. 'Winter Beauty' XII–II			Rose.
EUONYMUS *E. fortunei* 'Emerald 'n' Gold'	60 (2)	60 (2)	Excellent ground cover when grouped. A turbulent sea of silver and green which is particularly effective against a deep green background or an old red brick wall.
E. f. 'Silver Queen'	45 ($1\frac{1}{2}$)	60 (2)	Golden variegation.

Lavender hedge.

HEDERA *helix** Common Ivy			An excellent plant for ground cover between trees. A great many forms, with different leaf shapes and variegations, are available and should be seen.
HYPERICUM *calycinum** (St John's Wort) (Rose of Sharon) VI–VIII	45 (1½)	—	A creeping evergreen which does well in shade and can be massed by planting 45cm (18in) apart. Bright yellow waxy flowers with decorative stamens.
H. × *moserianum** VII–IX	45–60 (1½–2)	30 (1)	Spreading arching growth, large golden saucer flowers with reddish stamens.
H. × *moserianum* 'Tricolor'	60 (2)	60 (2)	Pink, cream and green variegated foliage; not very hardy.
LAVANDULA *angustifolia* 'Hidcote' VI–IX	45–60 (1½–2)	30 (1)	A neat bush with silvery foliage and a strongly coloured flower.
POTENTILLA 'Farreri' VI–VIII	60 (2)	45 (1½)	Foliage a pleasing green and finely divided. Flowers like large buttercups; is likely to exceed 60cm (2ft) but controllable.
P. 'Manchu' VI–VIII	30 (1)	30 (1)	A semi-prostrate mat of silver-green foliage sprinkled with the palest yellow flowers.
SANTOLINA *chamaecyparissus** (Cotton Lavender)	45 (1½)	30 (1)	Billowing silver-grey foliage out of which rise thin stems with bright yellow flowers. A good groundwork to set off a specimen.
VINCA *major** 'Variegata' (Periwinkle)	45 (1½)	—	A rampant spreading grower with cream variegated leaves and lilac-blue flowers. A splendid plant for banks and in semi-shade.
V. *minor**	15 (½)	—	Green foliage but generally a smaller plant than V. *major*. Good ground cover under trees though flowering better in the open; there is a variegated form and one with white flowers.

9 GROUND COVER

Ground cover in the garden is the equivalent of a carpet in furnishing a room and as much care should be taken in selecting suitable materials. Paving and gravel have their place, but when dealing with areas of cultivated earth prepared for the planting of trees and shrubs, we are more likely to look to suitable plants for ground cover, both for their aesthetic appeal and to control weeds.

Ground-cover plants control weeds simply by denying them the opportunity for germination. However, there is no magic formula: heathers are excellent ground-cover plants, but when they are first planted the ground between each one will be a perfect home for a weed; not until they have had time to form a mat will the heather plants choke out the weeds.

There are also occasions when ground-cover plants would be unsuitable. A bed of roses, for example, look well against a background of clean, cultivated earth and would suffer from the competition of a ground-cover plant. Since the use of the hoe can damage the roots, which then produce suckers, the best ground cover is a layer of pulverised bark.

Some taller growing shrubs can look after themselves as far as invasive weed growth is concerned, as they make a canopy down to the ground under which little will survive. Such plants include *Aucuba* (spotted laurel), some of the *Berberis* (barberry) family, *Cornus* (dog-wood), *Prunus laurocerasus* (common laurel), *Pyracantha* (firethorn), *Rubus* (flowering bramble), *Sambucus* (elder), shrub roses and (snowberry). The juniper *Juniperus media* 'Pfitzeriana', which can in time reach a height of 2m (6ft) and spread over an area 2.5m (8ft) or more in diameter, should also be included. Although this is not a complete list of such plants, these all have the merit of not being too fastidious as to soil and conditions.

Grass is of course widely used as ground cover, but it is not suitable for all situations. It is not unusual to find gardens where shrubs have been planted in very small beds or nicks cut in the turf. So often the shrubs are weakly, with whiskers of grass threading through them. They are denied air and moisture by the mat of turf and if the sites are enlarged the effect becomes spotty, and the mowing between even more tiresome. This is particularly pathetic when one finds beautiful little plants like Potentilla struggling for survival. Such plants are best planted in a mass in bare soil where they can give each other mutual support against weeds. We are in any case concerned more with ground-cover plants for flower-beds and for borders.

There are a number of small shrubs which will form a good mat at the front of a border. In the list on page 144, all the plants are fairly easy-going unless there is a note to the contrary.

Overleaf:

Left: Ground cover: *Cotoneaster horizontalis* in the foreground, with *Alchemilla mollis* behind, *Vinca minor* and the yellow flowers of *Potentilla* near the path; the bronze seedheads of *Euphorbia* and the silver of *Eryngium giganteum* 'Miss Willmott's Ghost' add further colour.

Right: Iberis (*left*), *Erica vagans* 'Mrs D. F. Maxwell' and *Vinca major* 'Variegata' providing good ground cover under overhanging juniper.

SHRUBS FOR GROUND COVER

Name   *notes*

Berberis
(Barberry)
B. candidula   The first two shrubs are low growing; although
B. wilsoniae   the third will reach a height of 1m (3ft), it is slow
B. verruculosa   growing.

Cotoneaster
C. conspicuus   Makes a mound.
C. dammeri   Absolutely prostrate: roots as it spreads.
C. horizontalis   Branches grow in the well-known 'fishbone'
                                    pattern.
C. microphyllus   Arching.
C. salicifolius   Has larger willow-like leaves.
  'Autumn Fire'
C. salicifolius
  'Repens'
C. 'Skogholm'   Wide spreading and arching.

Cytisus
(Broom)
C. × beanii   All these prefer a lighter soil and full sun.
C. decumbens
C. × kewensis
C. purgans
C. purpureus

Erica
(Heath)
E. herbacea   Gives good cover and is specially pleasing in the
                                    winter months.

Euonymus
E. fortunei   This is a big group of spreading varigated
                                    evergreens.

Hebe
H. pinguifolia 'Pagei'   This family does not like clay, but given sun will
                                    provide a number of cushion-like plants.
H. 'Carl Teschner'   Dark green hummocks with violet flower.
H. rakaiensis   White flower.

Hedera
(Ivy)
H. colchica
  'Dentata Variegata'   Soft green with yellow variegation.

H. helix 'Buttercup' *H. h.* 'Goldheart'	Small golden leaves. Green foliage with golden yellow centre.
Hypericum (St John's Wort or Rose of Sharon) *H. calycinum*	Billowing mass of green foliage, golden flowers in late autumn; spreads widely.
Mahonia *M. aquifolium* (Oregon Grape)	Has leaves not unlike holly, but thinner; carries a wealth of yellow flowers, followed by blue-black berries; spreads by underground suckers; very good in shade under trees.
Pontentilla (Cinquefoil) *P.* 'Elizabeth' *P.* 'Longacre' *P.* 'Red Ace'	There are a number of varieties, some of which can grow to 1m (3ft) in height, but these three small growing varieties are not only effective weed suppressors when close planted – 40cm (15in) apart – but can give the appearance of a gleam of sunlight.
Prunus *P. laurocerasus* 'Zabeliana' (Laurel)	This laurel has a slender leaf; it can grow about 1m (3ft) high, but can spread 2m (6ft).
Santolina (Cotton Lavender)	Provides a froth of grey foliage with a yellow flower.
Senecio *S. cineraria*	A well-known grey foliage plant which grows to 1m (3ft) in height; this variety has lobed leaves coated with white down and is a little tender.
Viburnum *V. davidii*	A beautiful foliage plant growing to 1m (3ft); its long, oval, deep green leaves are in themselves handsome and the female plant carries a turquoise blue berry.
Vinca (Periwinkle) *V. minor*	There are a number of suitable varieties, but this one particularly has small leaves and mauve primrose-like flowers in May.

Alchemilla mollis, with viola
in the foreground and peony
behind.

HERBACEOUS PLANTS PROVIDING GOOD GROUND COVER

Name	notes
Ajuga (Bugle)	Produces in June a forest of spikes of deep blue flowers. Some varieties have bronze metallic leaves.
Alchemilla (Lady's Mantle) *A. mollis*	A handsome plant whose plate-like leaves display tiny bubbles of water like diamonds on a tray.
Aubrieta	This little rock plant makes great mats of purple.

Aubrieta in foreground, with polyanthus and white hyacinth beyond.

Bergenia	A genus of beautiful plants with big round leaves and handsome, pink spikes of flowers in April.
Geranium (Cranesbill)	A number of varieties will provide plants for the front of the border with flowers in May and June as well as good autumn colour; *not* to be confused with *Pelargonium* (geranium).
Helleborus (Hellebore) *H. corsicus* (Corsican hellebore) *H. niger* (Christmas rose) *H. orientalis* (Lenten rose)	Creamy apple-green flowers from February to June. White flowers winter to spring. Various colours – white, cream, pink, purple – flowering from November to April.
Lamium (Dead Nettle) *L. galeobdolon* 'Variegatum' (Yellow Archangel)	This ornamental nettle spreads very easily; has very attractive silver-splashed foliage.
Lysimachia *L. nummularia* 'Aurea' (Creeping Jenny)	A beautiful plant: makes a golden carpet and looks splendid at the foot of any blue-flowered plant.
Saxifraga (Saxifrage) *S. umbrosa* (London Pride)	An accommodating plant which will stand sun or shade and is easily divided to increase the size of the drift.
Stachys *S. lanata* (Lamb's Ears, Lamb's Tongue)	A well-known grey foliage plant with leaves of a soft, felt-like texture.
Sedum (Stonecrop) *S. spectabile*	Pale grey-green fleshy leaves; when close planted the late summer flowers make a cushion of pink, which attract many bees and butterflies.
Viola (Pansy, Violet) *V. labradorica* *V. odorata*	Purple leaves; a charming 'natural' form. The scented, wild violet.

On a bank or a piece of ground calling only for cover, there are some coniferous plants which are both effective and beautiful; a few roses would also be suitable. Some suggestions are given below:

ROSES FOR GROUND COVER

Name	notes
Rosa	
R. *nitida*	Single bright pink flowers; leaves colour in autumn; spreads up to 60cm (2ft).
R. 'Paulii'	Has long, trailing shoots of single, white, scented flowers.
R. 'Red Blanket'	Grows up to 1·5m (5ft) and so would not be suitable for certain situations; small, semi-double rose-red flowers over a long period.
R. *rugosa* 'Fru Dagmar Hastrup'	Grows up to 1m (3ft); rose-pink flowers and crimson hips.
R. 'Max Graf'	Roots as it spreads; pink golden-centred flowers.

CONIFERS FOR GROUND COVER

Name	notes
Chamaecyparis (False Cypress)	
C. *lawsoniana* 'Pygmaea'	Has sprays of foliage which lie one above the other.
Juniperus (Juniper)	
J. *communis* 'Depressa Aurea'	Can grow 1m (3ft) or more across; has golden foliage; needs sun.
J. *c.* 'Hornibrookii'	Grows only 30cm (1ft) high, but spreads out to cover an area 2m (6ft) across.
J. *c.* 'Repanda'	Reaches 1m (3ft) across; has dull green shoots bronzing in winter.
J. *horizontalis* 'Emerald Spreader'	The emerald green foliage of this creeping form hugs the ground reaching 1·5m (5ft) across.
J. *h.* 'Glauca'	Blue-green prostrate grower more than 1m (3ft) across.
J. *h.* 'Hughes'	A plant of similar habit with grey-green foliage.

Above: Erica herbacea with in the foreground *Juniperus sabina tamariscifolia* and *Hebe pinguifolia* 'Pagei'.

Above, right: Juniperus procumbens and *Ajuga* 'Burgundy Glow'.

J. sabina tamariscifolia	Layers of foliage make a 'solid' plant 1m (3ft) across.
J. squamata 'Blue Carpet'	Particularly strong silver-blue foliage; can reach up to 2m (6ft) across.
J. virginiana 'Grey Owl'	Fine grey foliage up to 2m (6ft) across.

An area planted with such flat-growing conifers as those listed above will need some 'lift'. Conifers that can provide this include:

Juniperus squamata 'Blue Carpet', *Taxus baccata* 'Repens Aurea' and *Juniperus communis* 'Repanda'.

Name	notes
Chamaecyparis (False Cypress)	
C. *lawsoniana* 'Ellwoodii' (Lawson Cypress)	Grows only 2m (6ft) in height.
Juniperus (Juniper)	
J. *media* 'Pfitzeriana'	Starts as an apparently low plant, but reaches up to 2m (6ft), with branches at 45 degree angle.

J. squamata 'Meyeri'	Blue-grey foliage; grows with gracefully ascending branches curling over at the tips.
Taxus (Yew) *T. baccata* 'Fastigiata Aurea'	The golden form of Irish yew.
Thuja *T. occidentalis*	A stubby plant growing about 1m (3ft) high; gold foliage; a plant to place among soft greys.

10 SPREADING THE FLOWERING PERIOD

There is a great wealth of plant material to help in building up the garden. Trees and shrubs provide permanent structure and in this category we must certainly include roses. Many of the shrub roses grow to sizeable plants, giving height and beauty of form and foliage as well as bloom. The Floribunda roses which carry their blooms in clusters are also well suited to treatment as flowering shrubs in the border. The Hybrid Teas are best employed several of a kind planted in formal beds preferably fronted or surrounded by turf which shows them off well. There is no reason, however, why these, too, should not be used in the mixed border, especially in the small garden. Worked on 1–1·25m (3–4ft) stems they give us our standards. We even have perfect miniatures to grow in the 'precious' corner with the odd sentimental gems, in an old stone sink or on the top of a low retaining wall. The midsummer glory of climbers and ramblers, clothing fences, arches and other structures, is widely appreciated and needs no comment. Producing their main show in June and July with a second flowering to come, roses in the garden guarantee colour throughout the summer and well into the autumn. As to suitability for soil and climate, they do not *have* to have clay as is sometimes imagined, but they do like a good, cool, moist but well-drained soil, good air circulation and sunshine. If you are at all doubtful start with only a few.

Herbaceous Plants

Then there are herbaceous plants which for colour and decorative form are unsurpassed. They have a perennial root, but with stems and foliage which die down in the autumn to reappear the following spring. This raises two points for consideration: the growth being softer than that of most shrubs, herbaceous plants need support, and annual staking and tying is required, and the ground in which the plants are growing will be flat and featureless in the winter. Provided one is prepared to face the weeding between plants and the other tasks involved, a border or island bed devoted entirely to herbaceous plants is the most rewarding sight in summer, and in the larger garden the border can be placed so that it is not too close to the house or directly in front of the living-room window. In the little plot, probably all under the eye at one time, it is better to have the interesting form of shrubs in the winter and spring with herbaceous plants in groups among the shrubs to take care of summer colour.

Rousham Court: herbaceous borders.

Opposite: Cottage garden border, backed by a sawn-timber pergola.

Left: Water garden.

Alpines

Alpines or rock plants form a group – mostly small and miniatures – that provides valuable permanent planting. A little ingenuity will contrive some site if only for a few favourites: crevices in the paving, the top or face of a retaining wall, pockets between a few carefully placed pieces of natural rock. An old trough or sink of porous stone or even concrete (but not glazed) with a drainage hole and broken chips in the bottom to assist is ideal; even the flat-dweller can have a miniature garden on the window-sill or balcony made in a clay pan with a few flat pieces of stone against which two or three saxifrage or sedum with a tiny dwarf juniper can grow. As with herbaceous plants, it is wise to refer to specialist works or a good catalogue on alpine plants.

Aquatics

For those who introduce water in the form of a small pool there are aquatics, not only lilies and floating plants, but a lot of bog- and moisture-loving subjects for growing in the shallows. Goldfish, without which no pond is complete, become family pets and to watch their idle movement is said to be therapeutic.

Ferns, Pampas Grass, Bamboos

Nurseries also offer an array of miscellaneous plants such as ferns, a form plant so useful in the darker corners of the town garden for softening the effect of masonry, in shaded positions and for growing between trees and shrubs in woodland schemes.

Pampas Grass (*Cortaderia selloana*) with its arching sword-like leaves and great plumed arrows rising from the centre in the autumn looks fine on a lawn, but does create mowing difficulties and is better placed where it does not interfere with the mower.

Bamboos (*Arundinaria*) are very handsome plants, though some kinds are too massive for the little garden. A good choice would be *Arundinaria murielae* which grows to about 3·5m (12ft). Bamboos make a wonderful background and screen, and although they look particularly well reflected in water, they object to soggy land. Their greatest enemy is a cold wind.

Annuals, Biennials and Bedding Plants

This is a group of plants to which the beginner can turn with confidence. They are cheap, quick to give results, and, given good soil and sunshine, are easy to grow. The fact that they are temporary is an advantage in that each year you can try out new schemes, and if you are making a new garden you can use them for a season, have a clear-out in the autumn, fork-out weed which has developed despite your earlier efforts at cleaning, then plant with more permanent subjects. If you have your house on only a short lease this group gives you colour without the expense of permanent plants which you might have to leave behind.

Sow hardy annuals during March to May and the plant grows, flowers in about July or August and dies. Some of the toughest can be sown in September in southern Britain when they make a plant capable of withstanding a reasonable winter that flowers the following June rather earlier than those spring-sown. Examples of these are *Calendula*, Candytuft, Cornflower, Larkspur and Annual *Chrysanthemum* while the spring-sown annuals include such favourites as *Aly-*

ssum, *Clarkia*, *Nasturtium*, Sweet Sultan and Virginian Stock.

Half hardy and tender annuals have to be raised under glass and will only withstand our climate if outdoor planting of the young plants is delayed until about May. Examples are Tobacco plant, China Aster, Marigold, Pansy, Stock and Petunia.

Biennials sown in late spring make a plant that year, flower about twelve months after sowing, and then die, though in practice quite a number of perennials, e.g. Wallflower and Sweet William, are treated as biennials. Antirrhinum, Canterbury Bell, Forget-me-Not and Wallflower can be sown by the novice in May or June in rows in a reserve patch of garden, thinned to about 15cm (6in) apart. The plants have room to develop and can be moved to their flowering positions in October or the following spring.

Fortunately for the gardener with little time and space the half hardy and tender annuals and the biennials are grown by nurserymen and marketed under the broad term 'Bedding Plants'. Wallflowers, Canterbury Bells, Sweet Williams, and Polyanthus are available for autumn planting and, in May, market stalls and garden shops offer trays and small containers of plants. Also offered at this time are dwarf dahlias, the bigger dahlias, geraniums and so on, in pots at rather higher cost. The great advantage of bedding plants is the saving in time and the convenience of being able to fill in spaces in the border with plants which make up quickly and produce a blaze of colour.

Bulbs and Corms

Finally, there are the flowers which come from bulbs and corms; they cover the whole year and to most gardeners are a never-ending source of pleasure. Apart from books on the subject, the colourful catalogues offered by the trade on application are packed with useful information.

With so much to use, there is no difficulty in keeping a garden bright and colourful, especially from spring onwards, but even in the winter months it is possible to have interest. It is largely a question of getting to know your own garden, its soil and its most sheltered spots and remembering to provide in time for this period. Occasionally we have a winter which cuts down many of our most treasured possessions, but we also have mild ones when it is possible to pluck a rose in December, even if it is not as perfect as one cut in June.

Near the end of the year, when the first frost has taken toll of the dahlias and when the Michaelmas daisies and chrysanthemums are almost spent, we can look forward to the Christmas rose (*Helleborus niger*) and *Iris unguicularis*. With each frost more flame-coloured leaves will fall but the berries remain, the snowberry glistening white, the coral *Berberis* and the scarlet *Cotoneaster* and *Pyracantha*. The birds will take them, except for a few such as those of *Cotoneaster lacteus* which are spared for a while, and the tiny scarlet apples of *Malus × robusta* hang like lighted lanterns until February. The now leafless stems of the dogwoods (*Cornus*) glow crimson and gold after winter rain as though refusing to give in and become drab.

If you find something sad in this swan-song, at your feet you can find the little winter *Cyclamen* (*C. coum*) and a winter crocus (*C. laevigatus*). Here is new life and promise, and the winter cherry (*Prunus subhirtella* 'Autumnalis') starred with silver gives you back the flowers you thought you

Byworth Edge: mixed planting of shrubs and herbaceous plants.

Cottage garden with traditional flowers.

Anemone blanda and daffodils on the fringe of a country garden.

Trough garden.

had lost, the never failing winter jasmine lights up a wall face with its clear yellow, and in a sheltered corner wintersweet (*Chimonanthus fragrans*) can be cut to take indoors where a single sprig will scent a whole room.

In the shrubbery *Viburnum farreri* bears its fragrant flowers in profusion on the bare wood and a little later the evergreen laurustinus (*Viburnum tinus*), perhaps considered ordinary in summer, proves itself with a show of white, pink-tinted blossom.

The winter heathers are awake; *Erica herbacea* 'King George' is a cushion of pink later to be supported by *E. herbacea* 'Springwood White' and 'Springwood Pink', and standing among them may be the witch hazel (*Hamamelis mollis*) flaunting its little tufts of yellow ribbon.

With the new year comes the shy winter aconite (*Eranthis hyemalis*) and the snowdrop (*Galanthus nivalis*) growing in the grass or the edge of a border, followed by the miniature blue and gold iris (*Iris reticulata*) nestling on a sheltered rock shelf. *Crocus tommasinianus* will make a lilac drift between trees or shrubs in February followed in March by the blue Glory of the Snow (*Chionodoxa luciliae*), the ever popular purple, orange and white Crocus and *Anemone blanda*.

We are soon at the great spring show of daffodils, wallflowers, polyanthus and aubrieta, tulips and forget-me-nots, and are thinking of the dahlias to be planted for the latter half of the summer. All this takes scheming and you will find pleasure in doing it aided by good bulb and seed catalogues.

You may know a plant by sight, but not its name; you may know a name but be unable to 'give it a face' and a short cut to an introduction is an illustrated list. There are a number of very good books which will help but one of the most comprehensive, and well ordered reference is an erudite work by Roy Hay and Patrick Synge called *A Dictionary of Garden Plants in Colour* (Michael Joseph).

11 COLOUR THEORY APPLIED TO THE GARDEN

Colour brings a smile to the face of the garden, its warmth and vitality are the natural accompaniments to form. It is very much a matter for the individual and, as with music, there seems to be within us all some atavistic love of the subject which has long made it a form of self-expression. Again, like music, there are some who are naturally gifted and produce pleasing compositions as though by instinct; with others there must be some conscious effort, and on a few there is little impact.

No one, however, need be afraid that a poor colour sense will spoil his or her garden because we are not relying on colour alone. *Form comes first* and having taken care of that you should apply the colour boldly. After all, it is your own eye which will judge and it is *your* garden. If at first you make mistakes, a little transplanting and rearrangement will correct them.

You will find as you look for shrubs and trees with form that you can have colour too, not only in foliage – the reds, the greys, the variegated and the deep greens – but also in blossom. Remember we are not dealing with paint and flat surfaces, or dyed fabrics, but living materials in colours which are complex and subtle. One has only to look at a belt of woodland in autumn, a gamut of colour in perfect harmony, to realize that we can be free with the arrangement of foliage in the garden. Shrubs alone and the

flowers they carry provide an interesting exercise in colour arrangement and there is further scope for the enthusiast in the selection and grouping of border plants and roses.

It would be a mistake to say that flower colours do not clash; they often do. Much depends on the quantity as well as the quality of the colours brought together, the foliage background, and, possibly more than the colours themselves, the tones in which they are used.

Colour is a subject on its own and one too involved to pursue at any length here, but to explain tone and to help in deciding how best to employ colour in the garden, we must define a few terms.

Everyone is familiar with the rainbow which is white light split by drops of atmospheric moisture into its components *red, orange, yellow, green, blue* and *violet*. Imagine these set out in a continuous and everchanging band around a circle. There are no lines of demarcation between them: they blend gradually and evenly, producing innumerable gradations of pure colour which, because of its freedom from grey or adulteration, is at maximum intensity. The colour at any point on the circle is a *hue*, a term which denotes that it has a character of its own, a blue, for instance, as distinct from green or orange. Any hue, however, can vary in *tone*, i.e. its lightness or darkness, also referred to

The colour circle.

as high or low *value*. For example, while retaining its position as a hue, a blue can be diluted or whitened to the delicacy of an April sky, a lighter tone than the full hue and called a *tint*. At maximum saturation it is a *shade*. It can also take in grey in increasing quantities becoming a darker tone referred to as a greyed *shade* such as we find in the heart of a blue pansy.

Having taken in grey it can again be diluted or whitened giving a range of soft grey blues. So we have the intense (pure) and the greyed (less intense) hue in a wide range of tones.

We see a plant and its flower (or anything else for that matter) in colour because daylight falls on it and is either absorbed or reflected back to the eye. If *all* light is absorbed the object viewed appears to be black, if *all* light is reflected it is white, but due to the chemical make-up of the plant – the pigments contained in it – the light is broken up, some reflected and the rest absorbed. If the red part of light is reflected, the flower appears red; blue reflected gives a blue flower and so on, but usually, due to differences in the pigment, we have a number of hues reflected in varying quantity producing pinks, browns (a dark orange), olive green and greys. What we see as green leaves are not just green, but compounds of a number of hues shaded and veined and with a wide range of tones and textures. The red

Right: A garden planted with various tints and shades of orange and yellow to break up the outline of a cedar greenhouse.

Opposite, above: Warm colours (hues of red, orange and yellow): polyanthus and daffodils on the edge of a wood.

Opposite, below: White is assertive, whereas mauve flowers tend to recede into the background.

flower may have a sprinkling of yellow, the petals being shaded, blotched, finely veined or fading to white at the base, the stamens golden perhaps, and some of the flower red carried down the stem into the leaf. We see the balancing effect of the warm brown of soil and twigs, the variety of bark colours which on examination prove to be not a flat lifeless grey, but a rich combination of subdued colours and textures combining to produce a grey that is glowing and alive.

The result is similar to the comparison of a piece of self-coloured cloth and one woven with fine differently coloured threads. Not only does it give the vitality we know in living material, but seems to be nature's way of bringing under control and into a pleasing harmony hues which in dye or paint, applied by an inexperienced hand, would be discordant.

Strong pure hues are the most difficult to harmonize. As tints and shades and tints of greyed shades they are easier because of the presence of the grey, but the cautious can find harmony in closely related hues. Various tints and shades of orange with yellows and orange reds, i.e. between yellow and red in the circle, are safe; violet with red-violet and blue-violet and even red and blue are related, but are better kept away from the red to orange group.

Harmonious groups are 'pretty' but lack punch and you may like to use a contrasting hue with them. Perfect complements are found directly opposite in the colour circle and the choice can be widened by taking a hue with its complementary and the hues each side of the complementary, thus yellow with violet, red-violet (magenta) and blue-violet (indigo).

It is useful to know that the full hues in the colour circle are not equal in tone – they fall roughly into a tonal order. Yellow is the brightest, then working both ways round the circle the tone diminishes until violet, the darkest, is reached. White is brighter than any and black represents ultimate darkness.

If you plant two or more colours together and the result is not as pleasing as you hoped, question the tone by checking with the colour circle. Try to preserve the tonal order by using a light yellow with a deep violet rather than a dark yellow and pale mauve. An orange lighter than red is better than a powerful orange with pink (a pale red). A pale orange with a deep blue is richer than deep orange and pale blue. Keeping both hues of equal tone is preferable to reversing the tonal order.

The warm colours (i.e. those hues which contain red, orange and yellow) tend to assert themselves while the cool blues, blue-violets and blue-greens are recessive. This is of particular interest in the disposition of flower colour in the small garden when there is a wish to make the most of a small space. The assertive hues (including white) in the foreground with blues at the farther end can have the effect of increasing the apparent length of the garden though the position is reversed when looking back.

These observations on colour have avoided referring to primaries and secondaries or bringing in the difference in the behaviour of coloured light as against coloured pigments since this, though interesting, would only have confused the issue. Nature takes care of so much that our task of arranging flowers and shrubs should not be difficult; indeed, a great many colour effects will be pleasing because they could not be otherwise.

12 WATER AND ROCK

Water is still, as it always has been, a popular element in our gardens. In the very earliest gardens of the Far and Middle East the water hole was the focal point from which ran irrigation channels to supply the growing plants. This was no ornamental contrivance but a case of no water, no crops. Water has evolved throughout the long history of gardening: through myriad fountains which cooled the air, through the deep sequestered fish ponds of medieval monasteries, the jets and playful devices of the magnificent seventeenth century, to the still, artificial lakes of the eighteenth-century English landscape, to the little pond in the present-day garden. Here a jet of water still rises to give pleasure, a single water lily grows, and half a dozen goldfish gloat over their security as family pets. The fascination of water is universal and there are few gardens which need be without it in some form.

Water in the design must be sited with care; it is commanding and is best placed where it will not detract from a view, or lead the eye away from some other interesting part of the garden nearby. It can be effective as the hub of a formal arrangement of beds, the focal point in a paved court or in splendid isolation on the lawn, reflecting a blossom-laden tree or a silver patch of sky.

In a formal layout, the pool can be coped with stone, brick, tiles or similar material, either flush or raised above the surrounding ground. When a pool is surrounded by turf, a most restful effect is produced if the sides finish at ground level with what is best described as a knife edge, allowing the grass to grow right up to the water. There is a very good example of this on the terrace at the Royal Horticultural Society Garden at Wisley. This construction requires care and skill but is not beyond the amateur. A similar treatment of pool rim is desirable when the water is expected to look natural, since it would be false to line the edge with boulders or a continuous strip of flat stones.

In cases where the plot is big enough to allow some of the hard boundary lines to be lost, this 'natural' treatment of water can be pleasing, either making use of a single pool of irregular outline or a stream-like effect. The latter presupposes a little slope either existing or created, and since the watercourse must be kept full for best effect, the stream is in practice a series of level stretches with falls from one to the other according to the inclination of the ground. Such a system calls for the circulation of the same water by a small electric pump. This is a part of garden design which is best done on the site rather than on paper. Advantage can be taken of twists and folds in the ground where they exist and the work can be better visualized.

Arrange the line of the stream
so that you look down the
length of water from the best
viewpoint.

Plants in the surrounding
paving break up the severity
of line in this part of a
Kentish garden.

Formal pool with water lilies and small fountain.

If possible, arrange the line of the stream so that from your best viewpoint you look down the length of the water rather than across it; otherwise, the stream can become a slit or even disappear. You will find your best aid is a length of hose, rope, or even thick string, all of which can be re-adjusted until you find a line which satisfies.

It is well worth writing for catalogues of aquatics, offered in the weekend papers by specialist growers, and any books by Frances Perry, an authority on the subject, will fire your enthusiasm for water gardening.

To help you to decide whether or not to include a pool in your scheme, consider these points. On the credit side you have the added interest, the beauty of water lilies and other acquatics, the fascination of fish, and the sound of running water. Set against these the danger to small children, the possibility of fine leaks which defy detection and the practical consideration of cost. While you may be prepared to meet the cost of concrete or a fibre-glass prefabricated pool, there are odd extras which nibble at your budget. The pool can be filled from the mains, but in order to circulate the water you need a pump, the cost of which varies according to make and size.

To operate the pump, you will need a cable leading from the house. Armoured electric cable must be laid 45cm (18in) deep; the type of cable encased in a strong plastic, although easier to handle, must be laid on a bed of sand in a trench of the same depth. Even a good 'do-it-yourself' man would be well advised to consult a reliable electrical contractor, who is a member of a recognised trade association and conversant with the necessary safety regulations.

For small pools, there are very good little submersible pumps which can sit on a rock or on the pool floor; there is one so minute that it will give a sprinkle of water rising to a height of about 70cm (27in) and falling within a circle 50cm (20in) diameter. This

loggia

garage

Design for small, curved, formal pool, separated from a low hedge with paving. This feature is planned to divide the garden and provide a strip for vegetables. Behind is a more informal pool with a wavy edge.

would be suitable for a bowl on a terrace. At the other end of the scale, there are pumps either submersible or housed in a separate brick-built chamber that will provide a torrent of water to fall over rocks in an informal garden. The advertisement pages in any good gardening weekly will provide names of suppliers.

There are three modern methods of making a pool: by building a concrete pool, installing a prefabricated shell or by using a plastic pool-liner. The Cement and Concrete Association's *Concrete Round Your House And Garden* (for further details see page 101) provides helpful advice on ma-

king a concrete pool. For prefabricated and pool-liners, the manufacturers supply installation instructions.

Nearly all the garden designs in this book include a pool, for a well-designed pool will contribute beauty and pleasure to the garden.

ROCKWORK

Rock – natural unworked stone – is used in the garden in two main ways. One is for its landscape or scenic effect, where the material is employed in what is often termed natural outcrop which has been exposed by excavation or erosion. The aim is to create a balanced composition of form which simulates the natural habitat of rock plants, though when well done the composition is satisfying even before the addition of colour. The appeal is intensified when rock is used in association with water.

The Alpine enthusiast, however, interested in the growing of rock plants will look upon rock as a means of providing a suitable home for them, and though he is less concerned about the scenic effect he is equally careful about the placing of his stone, but with a different end in view. His rock will be sited and set so that it provides the shelter and sun and shade which a particular plant requires, and it will be tilted to drain rain water to the right place.

If the outcrop of rock is to look as though it belongs, it should be in indigenous stone or one which, to anyone but a geologist, looks as though it is at home. If your local stone-mason cannot supply you, he or your local nursery will be able to tell you of a source.

Before starting to build you should, if at all possible, give yourself a grounding by looking at what happens in nature. Then look objectively at the work of masters in the art of rockwork at the Chelsea Show or one of the other big provincial exhibitions.

Examine an exposed face of rock, perhaps in a quarry or on a hillside, and unless it is an igneous rock like granite you will see a suggestion or strongly marked lines of stratification. These are continuous and may be at any angle between the horizontal and vertical. These parallel lines show how the stone was deposited and grew in level layers, later to be thrown up by internal disturbance. Note the dramatic effect of steeply inclined strata, and the way in which a piece which has

broken off separates at a stratum line. This is important in that when we rebuild rock on a small scale these stratum lines must be parallel and the pieces of stone must lie on their proper bed.

You will often find that there is also some tilt in a direction at right angles to the strata lines, so that a piece of stone cropping out of a hillside slopes in two directions as indicated diagrammatically (*below*). This means that we can give the face of the stone a

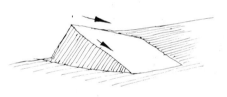

tilt upwards and the top of the stone a tilt back, though not necessarily at the same angle.

Behind the main face, there can often be found fine vertical fissures or cracks parallel with the main face, and crossed by minor cracks at intervals so that, when the stone weathers or is broken off, it parts at these faults, leaving another face showing parallel to the first. A cliff can present a number of such parallel faces.

Steeply inclined strata of rocks make a dramatic effect.

Stone outcrop sloping in two directions, shown diagrammatically.

Vertical fissures in the rocks of a cliff face.

Rock and water garden, with
small 'waterfall' in a
naturalistic setting.

Right: Pool in a small
suburban garden.

Opposite: Rock and water
garden (Douglas Knight
design for Chelsea Show
1982).

When rebuilding rock, faces
of the stones should lie on
lines parallel in plan.

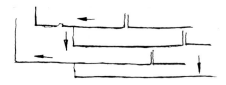

From this we learn that when rebuilding rock the faces of the stones
should lie on lines which are parallel
in plan. A diagrammatic section of
rock cropping out of a slope would
look something like the drawing
(*below*).

Section of rock cropping out
of a slope, shown
diagrammatically.

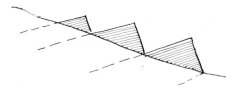

Now imagine an enormous bluff of
stone cropping out of the ground with
the inherent weaknesses mentioned

above. It might originally have been
shaped as below (*i*). Aeons of weathering and water might have removed
much of the softer stone, have cut
deep ravines in the cracks – which
would fill with grit – and have produced a terraced effect which can be
reduced to the simple lines of a diagram (*below* (*ii*)). Remembering that
you are condensing into your small
garden what nature often spreads over
acres, the above terracing rebuilt
would look as right.

Your observations from nature, the
parallel lines of the strata and the faces
of the rock are of the greatest value. It
is this orderliness which gives natural
rock its repose and dignity.

To apply your findings choose a
place for your rockwork where you
can give it a background of shrubs
and, if possible, small trees. Some
slope is an advantage and should be
contrived, if necessary, by remodel-

Right: A large block of stone
showing the laminations and
deep joints: an imaginary
bluff (*above*).

Weathering has given the
outcrop a terraced effect,
shown here diagrammatically
(*below*).

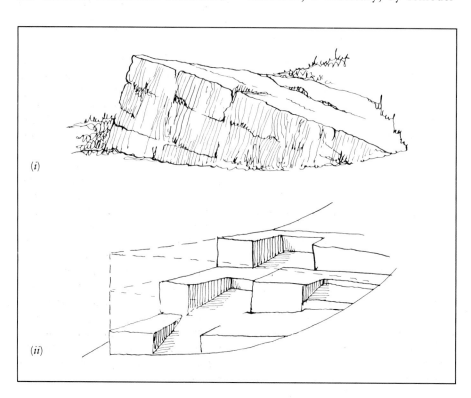

(*i*)

(*ii*)

The same outcrop of stone after planting. The outlines have also become softened.

ling the surface. The position should face south and/or west since most of the plants you grow among the rocks like sun and should have some shelter a little distance away to break the force of drying winds.

Buy stone in sizes you can conveniently handle. Moving them from the point where they are unloaded to the place of work is slow, but by hiring a few strong planks, a couple of crowbars and three or four short lengths of old steel or timber scaffold you can 'wheel' them into position.

Take your biggest and most handsome piece of stone and set it in a commanding position to become the focal point of the composition. Rest it on its natural 'bed' (not on edge), tilt it so that its top is inclined to the horizontal, twist it so that the extended stratum line would disappear into the slope and then give it a little back tilt. This establishes the direction and tilt for all the other stones. With string and canes you can mark lines which are parallel to the main face of this stone and which are running back into the slope at the same cant.

Select more stones to continue the face of the first and set them so that the top edge carries the line of the first. Stones placed close can often be made to fit so that they look like one.

Start a second face forward of the one now fixed, watch the direction not only in plan but in elevation. Avoid monotony and employ the bigger stones to give balance and strength to the whole. As you go, pack in soil and ram it to avoid air cavities and to ensure that every stone is firmly placed and not likely to topple if subjected to pressure.

Above, left: Alpine rock garden.

Above, right: The Hazels: rock garden.

Threave House: rock garden.

13 TOWN GARDENS

The little town garden, one of those tiny squares or narrow strips of land lying behind a tall terrace house in the heart of a town or city, presents difficulties, many of which are unconnected with its lack of size. It might even be said that, to some people, its restricted area is an advantage in that it saves work in much the same way as does the small house. This is true since any effort is concentrated and can be just so much more meticulous, and any materials or plants required can never be in great quantity so that there is an obvious saving in expense. Furthermore, it is possible to produce as peaceful a retreat within its narrow confines as in any large country garden, given the right conditions. The problems lie in these conditions.

What do we find? If we assume for a moment that the house is old, there will be remnants of an earlier garden, possibly a tree or a number of young sycamore saplings, a thicket of old privet, a laurel or aucuba, and laurustinus, and an odd accumulation of old stone and brick. The plot may be shut in by tall buildings, which not only make it look smaller than it really is, but cast dense shadows. These buildings may have windows at a high level robbing the site of privacy.

The soil is probably stale, impoverished, and structureless, either brick-like clay or fine dust and the air is polluted with smoke, dust and industrial fumes. There may even be only one way in – through the house, although a number of strange cats will find entry no difficulty at all. Not a promising start, but fortunately these obstacles are not always found together. Some can be altered and others mitigated, and the garden must be planned to suit those which have to remain.

These town plots can vary enormously in size, shape, aspect and surroundings and each will call for careful and individual attention. Deal first with the fundamental question and decide the purpose of the garden. You alone know the answer to this. Follow this by going through your own requirements. Is the garden something to be looked at from the house, a place into which you go only for its maintenance? In this case you will be creating a 'picture' or something rather like a stage set where the audience is not allowed behind the scenes. This can be intriguing and if you visualize your garden as a stage you will find yourself creating interest and a sense of depth with commanding plants at the sides of your setting rather like stage wings. You may even cheat by using smaller-growing plants in the distance than those in the foreground, dark colours beyond light, or by making lines which the eye expects to be parallel converge slightly (e.g. sides of a path).

If your viewpoint from the house is a high oblique, as from an upper window, you will be conscious of the ground pattern; and in winter particularly you will want to look down on pleasing shapes in a nicely balanced arrangement. In either case space required for movement will be confined to servicing and greater areas can be devoted to plants.

Perhaps you will have time to sit in the garden and, unlike the suburban and country plots where there is some latitude, your choice of an area for this will be restricted, and the chosen point may well become a nucleus for your design. It is no use devoting an area to chairs and table if it is in perpetual shade or is in full morning sun whereas your only free time is in the evening, if it is overlooked by neighbours' windows, or in such a position that conversation, except in whispers, is impossible. You will never use it. Consider also the question of access. If you are entertaining you will want to avoid a precarious walk with a tray; a site near the house might be better, particularly as it is within earshot of the telephone.

If your house is beautiful what nicer than to sit facing it? On the other hand, through no fault of yours, it may be quite ugly and then you are better with your back to it. These considerations – and you will be able to think of others – are often in conflict, and one must strike a happy medium.

A matter for early decision is that of the level of the garden, since some variation adds interest if it can be contrived. A way of doing this which immediately comes to mind is to sink part of it, but the temptation should be resisted until thought has been given to the dispersal of surface water which will inevitably collect in the lower ground. The presence of a fairly deep surface water drain which can be entered will satisfy the conditions, so

will the making of a soakaway (a deep hole packed with hardcore or stone – see page 69) in light or gravelly land, but on clay digging a sunken garden is inviting trouble.

When the garden is separated from the building by an 'area' there is freedom in the establishment of the garden level, but where it abuts on to the house the level must be clear of the air bricks or, as in all other cases, 15cm (6in) below the damp proof course. A slight fall over the garden site of even 30cm (1ft) can be utilized to create a shallow terrace, a change in level retained by a dwarf wall, or a raised bed.

A point easily overlooked is the disposal of garden refuse, which in the town can be quite a problem. Unless it is possible to dispose of prunings, leaves, mowings and so on outside the plot, some of the precious space inside must be devoted to a small enclosure where a compost heap can be made and an incinerator kept. When the

plot is long and narrow the farther end, perhaps not being the most suitable place for sitting, can be devoted to a few herbs and the storage and disposal of rubbish, and can be screened from the 'living-room' part of the garden by trees and shrubs. A plot with an irregularity in outline forming a minor appendage might be similarly treated, but you may be forced into taking a bite out of your flower garden for the purpose. This can be hedged in or hidden by a wall of bricks or ornamental concrete screen blocks, a fence or trellis or neatly framed panels of translucent plastic (see page 64). Such

Left: Utilizing a shallow slope to create a low terrace.

Below: Design and sketch of patio and pool for a small modern town garden.

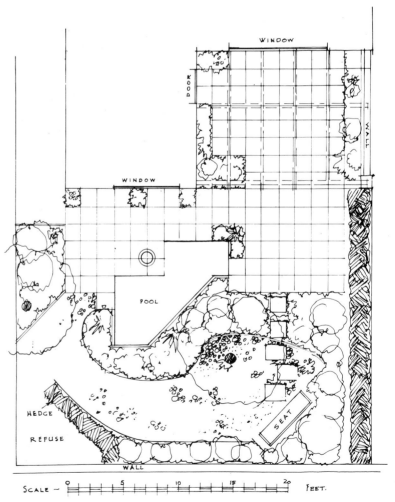

Trellis screen in a small town garden.

Opposite: A London roof garden.

Left: Azaleas provide massed colour in a terraced London garden.

Design for a town garden which allows for a 'right of way', screened by translucent fibreglass sheets framed in timber. The open framework of the sloping roof provides a partial screen against being overlooked by neighbouring upper windows.

Overleaf
Left: Clematis and ivy help to provide privacy in this London garden.

Right: The planting in this London garden creates a leafy oasis.

a screen being in full view will itself become a decorative feature when clothed with roses, honeysuckle and clematis. But this is going too far ahead. Though one needs to be forming a mental picture of the garden, you can see how easy it is to start thinking of the details before the main lines are settled. Having made an appraisal of the site and decided on the features you would like to include, can it be improved, and if so how?

First, think of aspect and mark for demolition any structure which it is possible to remove, and the removal of which will admit more light without destroying privacy. Examine any trees and, if necessary, arrange for thinning of the branches to the same end. This, especially in the case of big trees, is work calling for skill. But, expertly done, the tree will retain its balance and shape, cuts will be properly made at the right places and suitably treated. At all costs avoid the thoughtless hacking of branches, leaving sore-looking arms reaching out from a stump. They will break into

new growth, but the shape of the tree will be lost, and rot will set in at the jagged saw cuts.

One tree in the garden will probably be enough, but young sapling stems can be decorative, provided you remember that they will grow and, sooner or later, may have to come out. Do not remove shrubs or trees until you have plotted them on your plan unless they are so obviously in the wrong place that you know you will not want them. Those which have grown 'leggy' and top heavy can be cut back and a great many, such as lilac, privet and forsythia, will throw up new growth. If you have their positions on paper you will probably be able to work them into the new layout.

Since aspect is unalterable and you have done all you can to let in the maximum of light, the design must be adapted to the conditions, the best planting areas being sited in the sun, and the shadier positions styled for plants that like shade: ferns, hosta, lily of the valley, pyracantha, flowering currant, laurustinus, and so on.

While thinking of planting we must consider the atmospheric conditions, the smoke, grime and fumes, and it is as well to decide at an early stage to grow a limited number of permanent shrubs and perennial plants, to use bulbs and bedding out for colour, and to avoid the struggle to grow plants which will not tolerate the situation.

Generally speaking, deciduous shrubs – those which shed their leaves in the autumn – will be best, evergreens can be helped by constant spraying to wash grime from the leaves, and in both cases plants with glossy or smooth leaves will hold dirt less than those with hairy or crinkled leaves. Spiky foliage, such as iris and montbretia, washes clean in the rain.

Treatment of the garden surrounds

Left: A small town garden
where a trellis is placed
against a high wall and
another part of the wall is
white-washed or painted to
give an appearance of light.
On the left wall is a fan-
trained fruit tree.

Below: Another variation in
planning of a small town
garden of similar size to the
one above. Square shapes are
suitable for a small area.

will affect the plan. Assuming that the
plot is enclosed by walls or the sides
of buildings, it is worth considering
painting these, preferably in white, or
a light-reflecting colour. An ugly wall
perhaps festooned with pipes, or in
patched or clumsy brickwork, may
well be covered with a simple arrangement of posts or columns bearing tim-
bers running back to the wall. This
structure covered by climbing plants,
with the floor paved in cobbles or
brick with perhaps a small pool, or an
ornament or seat, may well become
the main feature of the garden, and the
rest of the layout would be planned to
lead up to it (*right*). The whole must
be treated as an extension to the house
where such a course is possible.

Often when an old building has
been rejuvenated there may be a big
floor-to-ceiling window, or doors to
the ground-floor living room. These

Wide doors from a living room lead into a small paved court in a town garden which includes one small tree and a pool.

are gifts to the garden designer, who can bring a little paved court right up to the windows so that, when they are open, the living room and court become one (*above*).

We can forget all attempts at hiding the boundaries, undulating lawn, bold shrub grouping, and what one might call 'naturalistic' effects. The scheme must be honestly man-made, which will not necessarily mean that it is stiff, square and symmetrical, or that we can depart from the principles of proportion and balance discussed in Chapter 1. Square shapes are restful, though curves and free-flowing lines can well be used, but they are the controlled and deliberate marking of decorative shapes, while the third dimension will be remembered in the provision of vertical accents.

These accents may take the form of an odd tree or shrub, or structural work such as a pergola. Bearing in mind the preservation of space, they will occur near the edge of the garden rather than at the centre. Rough in on your plan the main planting area which will have weight and need to be balanced with a tree or a shrub on the other side. Locate a focal point for the garden, perhaps a pool or ornament, in direct relationship with a window or door, or, when the latter is very

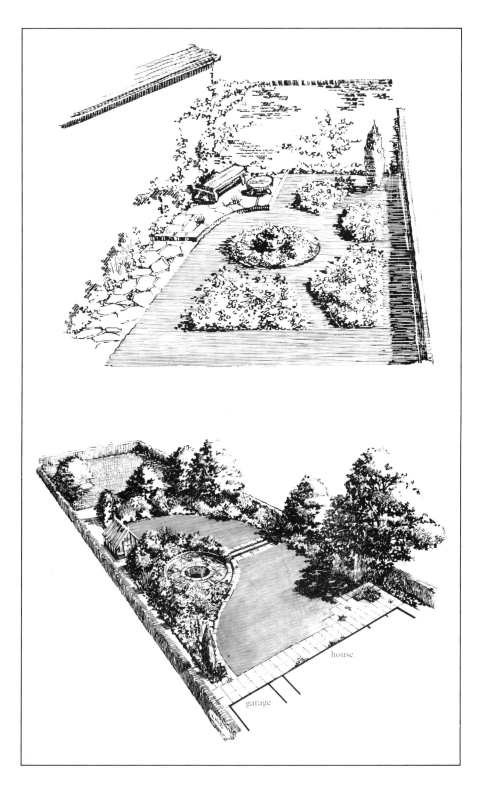

A small rose garden in a confined space. The grass paths are curved to allow easy mowing.

In this design for a larger town garden the greenhouse is screened from the house by the borders round the pool. The vegetable patch at the end is similarly screened.

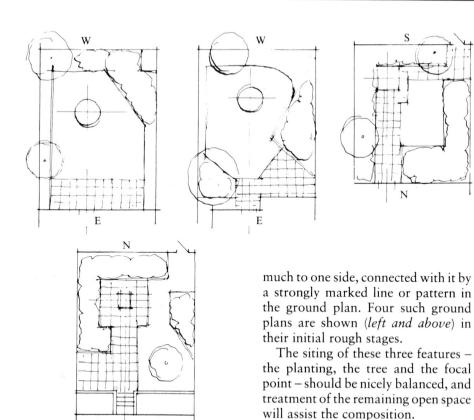

much to one side, connected with it by a strongly marked line or pattern in the ground plan. Four such ground plans are shown (*left and above*) in their initial rough stages.

The siting of these three features – the planting, the tree and the focal point – should be nicely balanced, and treatment of the remaining open space will assist the composition.

Above: Four examples of the initial steps in setting out an outline plan for a small town garden.

A small formal fountain and pool, edged with paving and gravel, are the focal point in this garden.

A formal pool in courtyard.

The words 'turf' and 'lawn' are practically synonymous, though it is in fact not necessary to think in terms of a lawn to make use of turf. Many a tiny town garden has no room for a 'lawn' but can have a small green carpet of grass used as part of a pattern in conjunction with some other material. If you want to include turf think of it in this way and shape it so that it is more or less entire and easy to maintain. Paving can occupy the remaining area and be relieved by planting or pattern where interest is needed.

A nice balance in a small semi-formal town garden between tree and seat, with a ground pattern of cobbles, paving and turf.

The four outline plans
developed further.

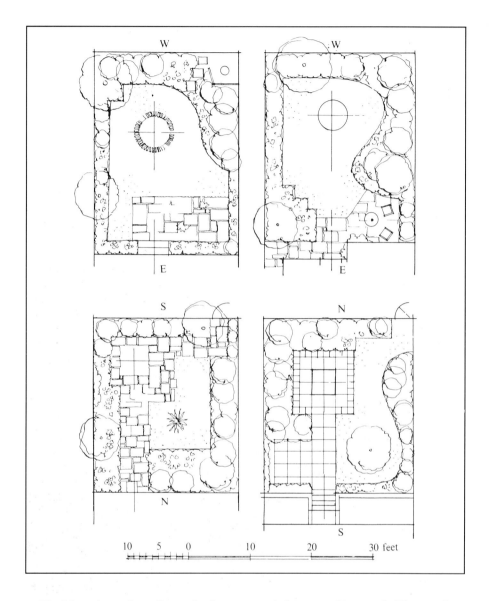

Working along these lines, the four initial roughs might develop as shown above. But do not over-elaborate; the material collectively is the essence of the garden. It simply needs grouping.

The whole process is rather like that employed in flower arrangement, and this might be said of the evolution of most small garden schemes. We have the container and the material, the main skeleton is worked out first and then supplemented. The result is balanced and restfully composed; it has contrast, harmony and rhythm. The growing flowers and foliage have intrinsic beauty displayed in nature's own inimitable way, but some of this is captured in a controlled and formalized rearrangement, except when there is a conscious effort to be 'clever'. That applies to garden design, too.

14 ACCESSORIES

Ornaments are used variously in the garden: they can be mere incidentals, or focal points or the centre of a whole scheme. The little accessories one adds to a garden are subject to individual taste, and it is important not to allow oneself to be too generous, and always to choose ornaments which are of artistic value. It is too easy to use figures which are out of scale, and an example of this is shown below where a miniature classical figure suitable for indoor use has been placed in a position where it is out of scale.

Almost anything can enliven a garden: an old trough, a carefully mounted bust or statue rising from foliage. An old chimney pot which looks so small when up aloft, and so enormous when down at ground level, may be found to have attractive decoration in relief and when filled with soil, be a home for trailing plants.

The main consideration is restraint: not only as to quantity, but in the artistic merit of the ornament used.

A newly made garden with a minature classical figure that would be perfectly suitable indoors, but is out of scale in this position.

A stone urn provides a focus
of interest in this corner of a
city garden.

Right: An elegant and
functional garden seat in an
Oxfordshire garden.

Opposite: a statue in a
London garden that is in
keeping with its surroundings.

Statue in a foliage setting.

Above: Design for a garden that has more width than length. The well is a genuine and original feature.

A whetstone used decoratively in a small garden.

Above: An original sculpture against a background of bamboo (*Arundinaria murielae*).

Above right: An old chimney pot used decoratively and to good effect in this patio garden.

Tatton Park: Victorian summerhouse with rose 'New Dawn'.

15 MAINTENANCE

The enthusiasm that often accompanies the making of a new garden will see us through a great deal of hard work which, at any other time, we should be loth to undertake. This is as well since there is much which can be done in the construction to save work later on. Once the garden is made we look for ways and means of taking the back-ache out of necessary and normal maintenance work, and it is surprising to discover just how much work is saved by buying the right and the best tools.

Two well-maintained – and easy to maintain – gardens.

Take a simple example such as mowing; no mower, however efficient, can be expected to work to capacity if its path is strewn with small beds, if the lawn has a tortuous outline difficult to follow, if it has an irregular surface and is edged with pieces of stone standing above the level of the turf. These are faults in the design to be avoided if maintenance aids are to be given a fair chance.

The following advice should help keep maintenance to a minimum.

Lawn

Essentials are: good clean soil, well firmed to a true surface, though undulation is permissible and often desirable; well-drained land to prevent stagnation; good seed, free of rye grass; areas as entire as possible, avoiding too many small beds; edges on easily mown curves, or lines avoiding indentations, scallops and wriggles. Avoid sharp tapering points of turf and narrow verges. Level of grass should be kept 4cm (1½in) or so above neighbouring surface.

Paths

Reduce paths to a minimum: make one path serve two purposes, i.e. avoid parallel paths where one will do. Keep level below turf. Make a good foundation for stability and drainage. Edge neatly with creosoted boards, concrete kerbing, or brick or stone strips on edge. Avoid edgings which are a home for weeds such as loose rocks or pieces of concrete. Clean ground thoroughly and apply weedkiller carefully before laying. Remember gravel needs weeding.

Paving

Lay paving over clean ground; if plants prohibited, or confined, lay with cement under each joint. Maintain a true level when laying. Avoid material which may crumble in frost. Keep stepping stones in lawn below turf level.

Planting areas

Thoroughly clean planting areas on bad land, delay permanent planting and use annuals or fallow the ground, in order to remove perennial weeds, and so eliminate forking between shrubs later. Do not use hedges unnecessarily; for example, where shrubs will form a satisfactory screen on a boundary the hedge may be omitted to save clipping.

To avoid seasonal re-stocking, limit the areas for bedding out plants. Remember that herbaceous borders, though beautiful, need care and staking. Where soil is suitable make good use of heathers, or low-growing plants like St John's wort for ground cover which inhibits weed growth.

Avoid too much spot planting in grass calling for hand-weeding of small individual beds.

Siting of essentials

Site the refuse corner, the tool shed if necessary, and the greenhouse in positions that avoid too much walking back and forth. One minute to empty the grass box or to fetch a hoe is a saving over three, especially when multiplied by the number of times such trips are made in the course of a morning's work. Place the linen line near the house. In the larger plot, consider a stand pipe half-way down the garden and tap for watering. Keep the service path to the vegetable garden as short as feasible and avoid too much cutting up of the latter with concrete, which interferes with the working of machines.

Level changes

Walls to retain a change in ground level need least attention. Avoid banks plastered with loose stones. When there is room, make banks at a shallow angle which will take the mower. Shape to a true surface neither sharply hollow nor humped.

Consider covering large banks with plants such as cistus, gorse, hypericum, and heather.

Attention to such points will eliminate a good deal of unnecessary work leaving more time for the essentials which are themselves sufficiently time-absorbing.

A lover of gardens spends time and money making one, not only because it will add to the value of his property, set off the house, and become a place for relaxation, but because it provides him with a spare-time occupation. In its care and the nursing of his plants is a satisfaction and contentment not to be found in any other way. In your case there will be greater incentive and greater satisfaction since your garden is of your own creation.

INDEX

Page numbers in *italic* refer to illustrations.

Photograph Credits

The author and publishers are grateful to the following for permission to use photographs:

Tania Midgley: pages 14 (top), 15 (top), 18 (top left), 18–19 (top), 26 (bottom), 34, 62 (top), 103, 107 (top), 110 (top), 115, 118, 138, 139, 146, 155 (top), 158 (top), 174 (top), 179 (top), 194 (top right and bottom).

Michael Warren: pages 135, 142, 143, 150, 151.

Harry Smith Horticultural Photographic Collection: pages 2, 6, 10, 14 (bottom), 27, 62 (bottom), 86, 98, 99, 107 (bottom), 110, 147, 154, 155 (bottom), 158 (bottom), 159, 163 (bottom), 166 (bottom), 167, 170 (top), 171, 174 (bottom), 178, 179 (bottom), 182, 183, 186, 187, 190, 191.

The author is particularly grateful to friends and clients who have kindly lent photographs: Tina Knight, page 18 (bottom); David Mann, page 26 (top), page 110 (bottom), page 193 (bottom); Helen Cronin, page 35; Penelope Roberts, page 70; H J Turner, page 102; Wendy Holmes, page 195.

All the other photographs are by the author, as are all the line and colour drawings.